Questions that You Will Be Able to Answer
After Reading this Book

Fill in the blank space in each question listed b̶e̶l̶... ̶
The correct answers will be f̶...

Chapter 1
1. You can preserve and collect animal tracks by making a (   ).
2. The track of a white-tailed deer will be a dainty (   ) hoof mark.
3. The white-tailed deer raises its "flag" as a (   ) (   ) to other members of its herd.
4. The raccoon hunts only during the (   ).
5. Raccoon tracks are easily recognized by their widely separated (   ) and tiny claws.
6. You seldom see a fox because its sense of (   ) is especially keen and it can run (   ) miles an hour.
7. Unlike most animals in the dog family, the (   ) can climb a tree.
8. Badgers, minks, otters and skunks all belong to the (   ) family.
9. A skunk can shoot its bad-smelling spray up to (   ) feet.
10. Skunks make (   ) pets.
11. Skunk odor can be removed from the skin by washing it with (   ).
12. The shy and wary (   ) loves to slide down mud banks.
13. The (   ) is a member of the same family as mice and rats.
14. The (   ) is North America's only marsupial.
15. Not all squirrels hibernate. Gray squirrels (   ) while red squirrels (   ).
16. Hares have (   ) ears and back legs; rabbits have (   ) ones.

Chapter 2
1. To find an owl, look for a (   ) tree with owl pellets or small (   ) scattered around its base.
2. The only proper time to collect birds' nests is in (   ).
3. The best time to look for feathers is in late (   ).
4. Not all feathers have color pigment in them. When they don't, they appear to have color because of (   ) light.

Chapter 3
1. An aqua-terrarium is a large glass

2. ... ̶o̶st̶ ... ̶i̶n̶ ̶this country.
3. S̶...̶m̶anders are the most primitive (   ) on earth.
4. The red eft becomes a (   ) when it goes to live in water.
5. Salamanders are (   ) lizards.
6. The stickleback fish will build a (   ) in your aquarium.
7. A fish rubbing is an (   ) or (   ) of a fish.

Chapter 4
1. Insects' skeletons are (   ) their bodies; the body is divided into (   ) parts, and they have (   ) legs.
2. Many insects have (   ) eyes.
3. The (   ) closely resembles a dead twig.
4. The song of the katydid can be heard a distance of (   ).
5. The (   ) can turn its head around and look over its shoulder.
6. Seeds of the dandelion and thistle are spread by (   ).
7. (   ) spread fruit tree seeds.

Chapter 5
1. The three kinds of rock are (   ), (   ), and (   ).
2. Most igneous rocks are made of (   ).
3. The impressions of ancient plants and animals left in rocks are called (   ).
4. Some (   ) minerals will glow with beautiful colors when placed under ultra violet light.

Chapter 6
1. (   ) is the property of water that permits objects to float on it.
2. An egg will float in (   ) water, but will sink in (   ) water.
3. Because of another property called (   ), you can make certain light objects sit on top of water.
4. Most sea shells are made by creatures called (   ).
5. The best time to hunt for shells is after (   ).

The QUESTION and ANSWER Book of
NATURE CRAFT

By **RICHARD F. DEMPEWOLFF**

Eastern Editor, Popular Mechanics Magazine

Illustrated by **DONALD VAN DYKE**

CAPITOL PUBLISHING COMPANY, INC., for

GOLDEN PRESS **NEW YORK**

Library of Congress Catalog Card Number 60-8638

COPYRIGHT © 1960 BY CAPITOL PUBLISHING COMPANY, INC.

All Rights Reserved

Published by Golden Press
New York

Manufactured in the United States of America

Third printing, 1963

Contents

Introduction:

Dr. Roy Chapman Andrews, late Director of the American Museum of Natural History, is the scientist-explorer who unearthed the rich fossil beds of the Gobi Desert and found the first known fossile dinosaur eggs. He tells about the importance of exploration—and how you can start right in your own back yard.

ACKNOWLEDGMENTS

No one knows so much about everything that he can write a book all by himself. Judy Dempewolff, my daughter, and her friend, Kit Powers, tested many of the projects in the book, and Judy researched and drew the animal tracks.

Mr. David Benglesdorf of the Pleasantville, N. Y. Junior High School Science Department suggested several ideas and devices for collecting and preserving insects. Many true stories about wild animals were provided by my friend, Pete Barrett.

Mr. Lewis Bowen, former president of Saw Mill River Audubon Society, contributed information on nest and feather collecting. Mr. Roger Eddy of Newington, Connecticut, who makes the Society's official bird call, suggested the bird call.

The formula for making Oriental fish prints was provided through the courtesy of the American Museum of Natural History. Jack M. Cooperman, Ph.D., Assistant Professor at the New York Medical College, advised me on several of the biochemical explanations in the book.

I am grateful to the Ford Times for their permission to use a number of curious items regarding various wild animals in articles written for the magazine by Pete Barrett.

THE AUTHOR

INTRODUCTION

Perhaps you've noticed how easy it is these days to speed past the interesting things that God created in the world around us. Whenever we go someplace, we climb in a car, zoom along a 60-mile-an-hour superhighway, then zoom home again. To go from city to city, we fly in 600-mile-an-hour airplanes. Soon, supersonic jets will take us on a world tour during a two-week vacation. That may be unique in its way. But Nature's wonderland will zip past us in a blur. The sad thing is that many of Nature's most curious secrets, unknown to many people, are hidden no further away than our own back yards, in the woods down the road, or in the stream at the bottom of the hill. But to see Nature in action, you must travel no faster than a walk.

This book takes you for a walk. It strolls through the woods with you looking for deer trails, animal tracks and dens. It shows you how to preserve and study the tracks you find. It browses through the forest with you, hunting for leaves to print, and stops here and there to help you perform experiments with things you find. You'll find directions for locating owl trees and the curious homes of birds and squirrels—to mention a few things. By following instructions you can learn to call the birds.

Along the marsh edge, you and the book can poke through the reeds looking for signs of marsh birds and animals. You'll discover how to collect creatures from a woodland brook, and how to keep them alive in a terrarium you can build yourself.

What the author of this book has tried to do is to bring a young "scientist's" dreams alive in a series of guided explorations that encompass a representative group of natural sciences. He has done it extraordinarily well, and I commend it to all nature-loving juvenile readers.

ROY CHAPMAN ANDREWS
Late Director
AMERICAN MUSEUM OF NATURAL HISTORY

Many people who finally get around to taking a walk or a hike are so busy going someplace that all they notice is which way the path goes. This is a sorry state of affairs, because the pathway itself, while convenient, offers the least interest of all the territory through which it meanders.

If this seems like an exaggeration, just go to the side of a woodland trail some day and scoop up a cupful of loose soil. It won't look like much in the cup. But if you spread it on a flat rock and examine it under an ordinary magnifying glass, you're in for the surprise of your life. Besides glittering multi-colored crystals eroded from Earth's rocky mantle, and spongy decayed matter that make up the loamy pile, you'll find it swarming with life. Anything from earthworms and grubs to ants, mites, and a wide variety of tiny insect eggs are sure to turn up.

The fact is that without a simple thing like soil there would be no life, as we know it, on earth. The soil is partly made up of bits of life on which a startling number of other things can live.

At the United States Department of Agriculture's experimental forest in Beltsville, Maryland, some scientists recently dug up a piece of earth ten inches deep and a yard square, after they'd sprayed the woods with a high concentration of DDT. They wanted to see how much insect life they'd killed in the forest, and how much was still alive under the leaves. In that small pile of soil, they found a mole, two mice, three spiders, five centipedes, 10 millipedes, 40 pill bugs, 50 snails and slugs, 3,340 worms of all kinds, 150 grubs, 160 fly eggs, 480 ants, 2,000 springtails, 20,000 mites, hundreds of rotifers and nematodes (*nem*-uh-toads), and 5,000,000 one-celled creatures called protozoans (pro-toh-*zoh*-ans). They didn't count the bacteria.

You can perform this experiment yourself. Take the top of a cardboard candy box or shoe box and cut a square hole in it with a razor blade, leaving a half-inch border to which you can staple an ordinary piece of window screening. With a straight-edged garden turf shovel, cut out a piece of untrampled forest soil to the shape and size of your sieve. It need only be an inch or two thick. Sift this through the screen onto a piece of newspaper. Crumple any clods with your fingers. On the first run you should have a good collection of bugs, along with pebbles too big to sift through. A good scientist will make a careful count of everything he finds, so be sure to keep pad and pencil handy. Remove the pebbles and count the living things. Now, look through the sifted pile on the newspaper for smaller things that went through. There should be dozens of mites—some so small you'll need a magnifying glass to see them. Count as many as you can and tally them on the pad. Don't forget to add in the little soft white insect eggs. To complete this experiment, do the same thing with a square foot of soil from an old cellar and see what you find.

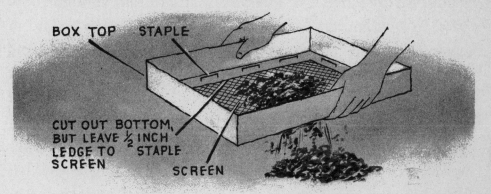

Now you have a small idea of the kind of thing you might tramp across on a hike without even knowing it—unless you're observant enough to take a look. And that's just one obvious example of the many curiosities that Nature holds in store for anyone interested enough to look around him.

So the best route to adventure on a nature hike is 'cross-lots. The nearest patch of woodland is a good place to begin. Wear tough jeans, a heavy, long-sleeved shirt, hiking shoes and woolen socks. Bring along a good knife, too.

Preserving Animal Tracks

Almost any patch of woodland in this country will have its share of larger inhabitants. Most are so timid you'll have to look sharply to see them scuttling away through the underbrush. But if you look in the right places, you'll find plenty of evidence of where they've been. Somewhere in the woods there's a small spring, brooklet or swampy area where these fellows go to drink. It may be just a shallow depression in the forest floor that puddles when it rains. The edges of such a place, in moist — but not too muddy — soil, usually are a gold mine of hoof and paw prints. You may also find them on damp, earthy patches of forest floor after a rain, though you'll have to look harder. Deer tracks, however, are easy to find in open woodland. These creatures of habit follow the same routes every day from the "yards" or clearings where they sleep, to the places where they drink and find their food: lichens, moss, tender shrubs and bark, acorns and the like. They soon create narrow paths through the low berry bushes and weeds. If you see such a faint trail skirting a wooded slope, chances are it was made by a small herd of deer. If you walk along it for a little distance, you may find many places where the print of a small cloven hoof has been firmly impressed in the soft earth.

Preserving and collecting such tracks is easy, and makes a fascinating hobby. You can cast them in plaster, the same way that detectives make casts of shoe prints around the scene of a crime.

The materials you need are simple:

1. A cupful of plaster of Paris.
2. A mixing bowl or tin.
3. A large spoon.
4. A couple of paper clips.
5. A soft 1-inch wide paint brush.
6. A strip of cardboard three inches wide and a foot long.

When you find a good, clear print, carefully brush away any debris found around it. Bend your cardboard strip into a circle, and fasten the lapped ends with the paper clips. Set this "collar" firmly into the soil around the track. Now pour some of your plaster of Paris into about half a cupful of water in the mixing container, stirring, and adding plaster slowly until the mixture has the consistency of pancake batter. Always pour the plaster into the water, rather than the other way around. Now pour the mixed plaster into the cardboard ring right over the footprint. In about half an hour, the plaster will have "set" in a permanent, brittle casting and you can strip off the cardboard and take home the footprint.

Why plaster behaves this way is a curious function of nature in itself. Plaster's natural form is gypsum, a soft crystal-line rock that occurs in many grades of color and texture. One of them we know as alabaster, a beautiful translucent rock with white, pink and gray shadings. Ancient Easterners made alabaster famous in many objects of art such as vases and sculptures. Gypsum is nothing more than a natural combination—of all things—of calcium, sulphur and oxygen, held together in a crystal-like structure by tiny molecules of water. To make plaster, men heat gypsum in ovens so that most of the water evaporates. With fewer water molecules to hold its crystals in shape, the beautiful gypsum crumbles into powder, which is ground into the fine plaster flour you buy in the store. When you add water to it for your mold, you are replacing the water that was baked out of it. As the water molecules combine with the plaster, the baked gypsum immediately begins to crystallize again, assuming a form very similar to its original one—a fine, close-grained brittle material, whiter than alabaster and smooth to touch. The growth of crystals is a wonderful thing to watch, and we'll get back to it in a later chapter that tells you how to grow your own crystal "garden."

> A nice thing about plaster is that it takes kindly to water colors, so you can paint colored backgrounds around the hoof and paw prints you collect, and hang them on the wall of your room to add a decorative touch. Be sure to label each one carefully, comparing it closely with the sample prints shown on these pages to make sure you credit it to the proper animal. If you're in doubt about any, check them with a biology teacher.

What kinds of animals can you expect to find in suburban and semi-rural woodlots everyplace in the United States? There are 3,622 known kinds of mammals in North America, many of them found only in certain regions. But quite a few, common to nearly all areas, are certain to reveal themselves —or their signs—if you search carefully. It's easy to find evidence of their whereabouts if you know something about them and their habits. So, let's take a look at the private lives of a few forest dwellers who can be found in virtually every state in the Union.

The White-tailed Deer, also called the Virginia deer, is one of the most graceful and dainty of all creatures. He ranges from Canada to Texas. A big one may weigh 280 pounds. He's a member of the Cervidae (*Sir*-vih-dee) family. Like their Bovidae (*Bo*-vih-de) cousins, cattle and sheep, deer have cloven hooves (see diagram), a complicated stomach with four compartments, and they ruminate, or chew their cud. The white-tail's name comes from the patch of bright white fur on the underside of his tail, which any farmer will tell you is his "danger flag." When he's startled, that tail goes erect, and the other deer in the herd can see the flashing signal. One by one, the other flags pop up, and stay erect as the creatures bound away with spectacular spring and buoyancy, sometimes clearing eight or ten-foot obstacles in a single leap.

WHITE TAILED DEER

HIND FOOT PRINT

If you're an early riser, you can treat yourself to an exciting experience some morning by hiding near a deer trail half an hour before sunrise. On a well-traveled trail, deer tracks and other spoor are distinct—there are usually fresh droppings (that resemble small clusters of black jelly beans). This is a major thoroughfare from the "yard" to a feeding or drinking spot. The trick is to remain absolutely motionless, with your back against the trunk of a big tree—down wind from the trail. Deer have highly sensitive noses. Pretty soon, if you're lucky, you'll hear the *shh-shh-shh* of tiny hooves stirring the leaves on the forest floor, and a moment later they'll come into view—single file, as deer always travel in open forest. First will be a doe, then another and another with the buck bringing up the rear, where he can take off like a boy on a pogo stick if any of his wives up front run into trouble and fly the danger flag.

You'll be amazed at how close these wild things may come if you remain perfectly still. Bright colored clothes won't startle them, but a wisp of vapor from your breath on a frosty morning will send a herd exploding through the woods. On an icy December morning, I have had the first doe in a column stand within ten feet of me before she caught a movement in my eyes. Her flag went up. She stared straight at me, expecting me to move. When I didn't, she stamped a tiny hoof in the leaves several times, to see if that would startle me into action. Then she turned away and suddenly sprang back to see if I'd moved when her back was turned. Finally, still suspicious, she trotted off, looking back over her shoulder several times enroute.

Few wild animals fare better in captivity than the White-tail. Fawns quickly learn to take milk from a bottle and, as they grow, will accept almost any kind of vegetable diet. They seem to enjoy domesticity, and soon lose their timidity.

For this reason, many states have passed laws prohibiting people from making pets of deer. Sooner or later, the deer grows too big to keep and is turned loose. Since timidity is his main protection against enemies, a domesticated deer won't survive long in the forest. So, as good as your motives may be, it's better to turn a lost fawn over to the conservation authorities rather than to care for him yourself.

The Raccoon Family. If any forest creatures besides the fox (which we'll come to) can be described as "bright-eyed and bushy-tailed", the raccoon and his first cousin, the ring-tailed

HIND FOOT PRINT

RACCOON

cat, are the ones. Though the raccoon's stamping ground includes only North and Central America, he can be found nearly everywhere in that habitat. Generally he avoids dense, deep forests, preferring the open woods near civilization, where he can sneak into chicken pens occasionally for a mouthful of feathers or eggs, and knock the lids off people's garbage pails for a midnight snack. Nature has equipped this crafty fellow with appropriate markings for this sort of mischief. Besides the characteristic row of black rings around his tail, every raccoon has a perfect black "bandit" eye-mask across his white, sharp-nosed face. The little animal, slightly larger than a cat, also feeds abundantly on crayfish, mice, turtles and their eggs, frogs, fish, fresh-water mollusks and young birds, which he varies now and then with fruits, nuts and corn.

Although he is a first-rate climber, and usually makes his nest high in a hollow tree, the raccoon does all his hunting and cavorting on the ground at night. The best way to see him is to prowl his haunts with a flashlight at night.

Since raccoons spend a lot of time near water, and are excellent swimmers, they're great candidates for footprint plaster casts. Along any stream or brooklet someplace you will find the prints of a raccoon who's been crouching on the bank, scooping out fish with his front paws. You can't miss the marks of his widely separated pads and tiny claws. Like bears and humans, he walks in plantigrade fashion, which means that both the heel and sole of his feet touch the ground. In fact, Indians called the raccoon "the little brother of the bear." He also has an appealing way of using his front paws like hands, and often likes to wash his food in the nearest stream or puddle before he eats it.

These forest dwellers are easily domesticated, and make amusing pets. They frequently attach themselves to people who leave food out for them regularly.

Foxes. The chance of running across a fox on a woodland hike is slim. That's not because there aren't foxes in your area. There's hardly a state in the union, except Hawaii, that doesn't have a sturdy population of either red or gray fox— the two common varieties. But this sly member of the dog family hasn't earned his reputation for craftiness and speed for nothing. If you're a constant hiker across fields and countryside, you may some day catch a glimpse of a flying bundle of fur, some three feet long, tearing by close to the ground in high grass. That will be a fox—on his way elsewhere. He undoubtedly heard you coming, because his hearing is exceptionally keen and he uses it in his business more than he does his sight. The red fox of the northeastern states has been clocked at 40 miles an hour.

GRAY FOX   RED FOX   HIND FOOT PRINT

The den, or "earth," of a red fox is easy to identify if you find one. It may be a roomy hole he has excavated himself, or an abandoned hole adapted to his needs. He usually carves a chamber beyond the den itself for a storehouse. In either case, the ground around it will be littered with bits of fur, feathers and bones of the things that foxes eat. These include woodchucks, rabbits, mice, partridge and occasionally domestic poultry.

The true gray fox has a less distinctive den. Usually a rocky overhang or hollow log will do for him, but you'll find the same signs around his lair. He's smaller than his red cousin, and less crafty, but the gray fox has a unique distinction.

When run hard by hounds he will head for a hollow tree, and either crawl in it—or climb it! Unlike most animals in the dog family, he can scamper up a tree with the agility of a cat. Look for his tracks in soft earth along hedgerows and woods bordering the fields.

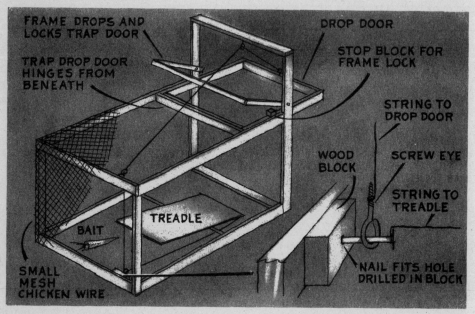

You can learn a great deal about small wild animals by setting up a live animal trap. The cage-trap diagrammed here is simple to make of one-by-two-inch lumber and small-gauge chicken wire. The trap door, which cannot harm even the most delicate animal, is easily lifted by a string from behind the cage, so that the animal can be released without handling him. This is important, since even a wild rabbit can inflict a painful bite if he's frightened. Under no circumstances should you ever handle an untrained wild animal. This is for expert professionals.

Lettuce, a scrap of meat, and peanuts should bring some hungry wanderer into your cage if you're patient.

The important thing to remember is that these are wild creatures, and many of them die quickly in captivity. Even a raccoon is difficult to domesticate in a cage. So a good rule of thumb is never to keep any wild animal in a cage for more than a day. But if you stick to that rule, you can make many interesting discoveries about small forest dwellers. Feed them tidbits of the things that comprise their normal diet, and watch their behavior. If an animal refuses to eat, or seems nervous or sad, let him out immediately. Another more sociable fellow may investigate your bait tomorrow.

The Weasel Family includes badgers, minks, otters, skunks, martens, wolverines and weasels. The clan is called "Mustelidae (Mus-*tel*-ih-dee). They are a small, bloodthirsty lot, by and large—distinguished by musk glands that give them a remarkable odor. In the case of the skunk, the odor is remarkable enough to be famous. The entire family walks sometimes on the soles of their feet, and sometimes on their toes, making them both plantigrade and digitigrade (*dij*-ih-tih-grade). It also makes their footprints hard to distinguish until you're used to them. Three members of the family live close to civilization and are worth scouting for.

The weasel himself is a long, slender and graceful animal who comes in a variety of colors and sizes, ranging up to 16 inches long. In summer his coat may be golden brown; in winter he matches the snow, save for the jet black tip on his slim tail. He's a lithe bundle of muscle, bold and curious. You're likely to see him poking his sharp nose from a cranny

HIND FOOT PRINT

WEASEL

or hole in the woodland floor to stare at you fearlessly if you pass close to his den. I met a weasel on a path not 100 feet from my house one day. He sat there on his haunches swaying back and forth and watching me with an angry green glitter in his fierce little eyes—like a cobra ready to strike. He

21

couldn't have been more than a foot long, including his tail. Yet there wasn't much doubt that he expected *me* to get out of *his* way.

A weasel's nest usually consists of a bed of leaves in a hollow log, or the diggings of some other creature he has chased out. A small hole in the ground with bits of fur or feathers nearby will almost surely be a weasel's lair. Look for his footprints, too. If you find some good ones, this is an excellent site to set up the camera trap described on page 29.

Skunks can be a lot of fun. It's true that even the most fearless animals, such as bobcats and bears, will carefully pick their way in a wide semicircle around a skunk. The most common member of the family is the striped skunk. This handsome black creature, with a broad white stripe down his back, is treated like a walking time bomb by all the forest folk. And with good reason. The skunk's "ammunition," fired through ducts leading from two small glands beneath his tail, consists of only three drops of amber fluid which he can eject in a fine spray for distances up to 15 feet. Yet it will "perfume" the air for half a mile in every direction.

You've probably heard, as I have, that skunks wet their tails with the foul concoction and *flip* the juice at enemies, or that they squirt it from holes near the nose. Neither is true. Actually, skunks are among the cleanest of all animals and wouldn't dream of soiling themselves. When a skunk fires, his tail plumage is held well clear of the stream. If a skunk is facing you, there's nothing to fear. But if he lifts his tail erect and turns around—watch out!

Skunks act thoroughly assured of their invincible power. You'll seldom find an old one who isn't fat. He's never had to run. The typical skunk in his native woods is a plump ball of fur ambling along with amiable indifference, minding his own business. He may pass within a few feet of you, stopping to sniff here and turn over a stone there, totally preoccupied. Obviously, he knows he can handle you if need be.

My friend Pete Barrett, a great outdoorsman, told me about watching a skunk and a bull squared off in a New Hampshire field one morning. The bull snorted and pawed the ground in good blundering bull style. Only a few feet away, the skunk, eyeing him disdainfully, would calmly move a few steps closer to a nearby rockpile every few seconds. "Well," said Pete, "you know how bulls are. This one got too brave. The skunk turned. Up went his tail, and the spray hit the bull square on the nose from five feet. The bull rushed off bellowing in agony. The skunk calmly ambled away as though nothing had happened."

SKUNK

HIND FOOT PRINT

Skunks make wonderful household pets. If captured young and petted often, they'll exhibit more affection and playfulness than a cat. They are easily housebroken and can even be taught to come when called. Though several of my friends claim to have kept fully armed skunks without disastrous results, the recommended procedure is to have the armament removed. Most veterinarians are equipped to do this for a small fee. Today, you can buy a disarmed skunk for about $25. But you can trap your own if you have the courage and know where to set up your gear. Look for his tracks or his den. Skunk tracks are easily identified. His ambling gait, half hop, half walk, creates paw prints in a series of diagonal lines in soft earth. (see diagram). He usually lives in a burrow, which he may carve with his own claws or adapt from a woodchuck hole, a cave, or hollow log. Inside is a bed of grass and leaves, where six or eight young are born in the spring.

If you care to take a night hike in almost any suburban wood during late spring or early summer, you're quite likely to see a skunk family bobbling along single file, mother in the lead, youngsters stretched out in a line 15 or 20 feet long behind her.

In spite of what I've said about his amiability, sometimes it doesn't take much to anger a newly captured skunk. Peter, Robert, Michael and David Gonze, the four young sons of our Pennsylvania neighbors, trapped a live skunk recently. Their mother, a lady of courage, volunteered to try feeding it for the boys with disastrous results. By doing a little research, however, she discovered that she could remove the skunk odor almost entirely by washing the tainted areas of her skin with canned tomato juice. It's a good thing to remember because it works for very sound chemical reasons. Skunk juice contains a chemical called "butyl mercaptan," which is the same thing that chemists put in odorless natural gas so people can smell gas leaks. The only pleasant thing about it is that, when certain other chemicals touch it, butyl mercaptan quickly oxidizes. Oxidation is really a very slow version of burning. When wood burns, it is oxidizing. When steel is near salt water, it oxidizes —or rusts—quickly. The same thing happens to butyl mercaptan when the vitamin C in tomato juice touches it. And in the slow "burning," or oxidation process, the smelly molecules "go up in smoke," so to speak.

Anyway, trapping and training a baby skunk can be fun if you—*and your family*—are willing to take the possible consequences. Good luck!

Otters are shy and wary. We have an otter family in our community lake, no more than 100 miles from New York City. Yet they've only been seen twice in as many years although some 30 families use that lake. Otters have been reported in the city reservoirs only 20 miles from New York, and are seldom seen. Almost any body of clean fresh water, with abundant fish, is good territory for this big fellow. Nearly 40 inches long, his brown streamlined body, webbed feet and powerful tail (which he uses as a rudder), make him ideally equipped for a life in the water. His home is entered through a hole in the bank, beneath the surface. It consists of two or three rooms, high and dry above the water line. Leaving this hidden cave, he moves under water with the speed and grace of a seal to catch a dodging trout in his steely jaws. Hustling back with it to his home, or a secluded spot ashore, he holds his prey in his forepaws and eats it. Hardly a sign shows anywhere to tell he is in business. Besides fish, he likes frogs, shellfish, eggs and occasionally water fowl.

In spite of the care he takes to hide his tracks, you can find signs of the otter's whereabouts if you know what to look for.

Look closely along the banks of lakes and large streams for web-footed paw prints in the mud, and for slick, troughlike slides on steep embankments.

The otter's greatest pleasure in life is playing shoot-the-chute with his family on a river bank. Picking a steep site, mother and father otter, plus two or three half-grown youngsters, will take turns crossing their forepaws in front of them and sliding headfirst down a muddy bank into the water. They'll keep up such a performance until the slope is slick as glass from their smooth under-fur. My friend Pete Barrett tells about watching five members of an otter family follow each other into a foaming, rock-studded Idaho cascade. Plunging into the water with a loud *smack*, they'd swim full-tilt

MUSKRAT   OTTER

HIND FOOT PRINT   HIND FOOT PRINT →

downstream through the raging millrace, then scamper ashore and hurry back up the bank for another try. They kept it up for half an hour.

If he isn't riding his private roller coaster, the otter has a dozen other pastimes to satisfy his playful nature. Families rough and tumble on the river banks, play tag or catch with clods of earth or anything handy.

Despite his shyness, the otter is highly intelligent and can be readily domesticated—if you can catch a young one. A well known sportsman had four of them some years ago. He trained them so successfully that they'd come running when he whistled, and would work for him by retrieving ducks that he shot each fall.

The Muskrat is another lake or pond dweller who leads an exclusive life, but is not nearly as shy as the otter. He is, actually, nothing more than a great mouse with the instincts of a beaver. His family, called "Muridae" (*Mew*-rih-dee), includes rats and mice. Almost any reasonably quiet pond will suit him, and his haunts are easily identified. My daughter Judy and I, fishing in our lake at that quiet time of evening when the glassy-smooth water is seldom ruffled by anything but the *smack* of a trout leaping for a fly, have spied the wedge-shaped heads of our muskrat neighbors cutting a pattern of angular wakes from shore to shore. Ghosting silently through the black water, they frequently carry sticks, straw, bark and other debris in their oddly shaped mouths. This material is for the muskrat houses and home-made "islands" of trash that they are forever bolstering and re-building back in the cove. The muskrat—which also goes by the name of "musquash"—is a first class "safety-firster." His floating islands are anchored in place by the cattails and rushes growing around them. He uses them to sit on when he eats or rests. There, enemies can only get to him from the air. When attacked, he simply plops into the water.

Muskrat winter houses are easy to spot. Look for mounds of trash and mud poking through the surface from the pond's bottom. The animal makes these by building a pile of mud and weed stalks in shallow water about two feet deep. From the bottom of this submarine tower he bores a tunnel upward, hollowing out a small dry chamber above water level.

In summer, the muskrat lives in a labyrinth of tunnels that enter the banks of the pond beneath the water and wander upward to cavities beneath the tree roots. Along the edge of a muskrat pond, you may find half a dozen small ventilation holes leading down to his tunnel.

Rig A Camera Trap For Night Animals

Night prowling animals like raccoons, skunks and 'possums can be caught unaware, and permanently preserved on film, by rigging a camera trap and letting them take their own pictures. Collecting wild animal photographs is not just an unusual hobby. Photography is an important aid to all scientists, and it's good to learn as much as you can about it.

The best kind of camera for this work is a cheap box camera with flash attachment. The simple shutter trigger on a box camera makes it easier to set up than more expensive kinds. Furthermore, the trap will be out in the woods unattended, and an expensive camera might be tempting to passers-by. Here's the equipment you need:

1. Flash type box camera with film.
2. A single mouse trap.
3. Strong, heavy gauge thread.
4. A wooden stake one foot long.
5. One large screw eye.
6. Leather straps or twine to tie camera and trap to a tree trunk.
7. Bait.

First, you will have to drill a tiny hole part way into the camera's shutter release, and fit a little screw into it with the head projecting, so that you have something to which you can tie the end of the thread. Tape or tie the camera and mousetrap to the tree as shown in the diagram. Then, with the mousetrap set, tie the other end of the shutter thread firmly to the trap's snap bar, with enough slack so that when the trap is sprung the

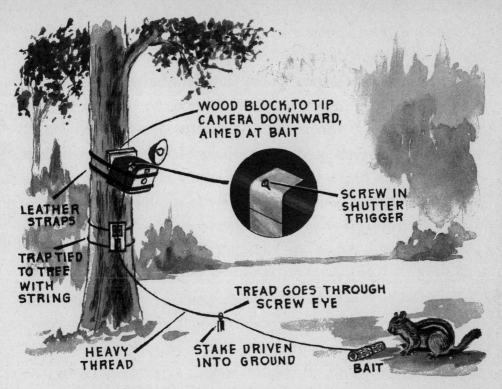

WOOD BLOCK, TO TIP CAMERA DOWNWARD, AIMED AT BAIT

SCREW IN SHUTTER TRIGGER

LEATHER STRAPS

TRAP TIED TO TREE WITH STRING

TREAD GOES THROUGH SCREW EYE

HEAVY THREAD

STAKE DRIVEN INTO GROUND

BAIT

string will trip the shutter but will not be too short to keep the trap from closing. When you do this, have someone hold the snap bar open.

Now drive your stake into the ground near the base of the tree, until only two or three inches of it stick out. Fasten the screw eye in the top of the stake as shown. Tie a six-foot piece of thread to the bait tab on the trap. String the thread through the screw eye, lay out four or five feet of it along the ground, and tie your bait on the end.

Don't forget to sight through the camera finder to be sure the lens is aimed properly, and that the camera will see all of the animal whose picture you want. Protect the camera against rain with a piece of plastic sheeting, or a cardboard roof, taking care not to cover the lens. Now set the mouse trap, and the trap is ready for the first bait nibble.

Though a camera trap can be located almost anyplace along a woodland trail with good chance of success, you'll do better if you place it where you've found some animal tracks or signs. If you want a picture of a deer, woodchuck, or skunk, set up your rig along the edge of woods near a field or pasture. Raccoons and weasels may take their own pictures more frequently along the stream banks where they come to drink. Along the shores of a lake or pool, you may snap a muskrat or an otter. Be sure you set out the right kind of bait if you're after a picture of a particular animal. Fresh raw meat, for instance, is tempting to weasels. Raccoons, skunks and opossums also like meat, and corn on the cob, too.

The Opossum is a genuine American curiosity. You'll find him in almost any small patch of woodland in this country. His family name is Didelphidae (Dy-*del*-fih-dee). Only a few years ago, the 'possum was considered an animal of the Southland. But he's been migrating north. Recently, 'possums have even been seen in great numbers as far north as Ontario, Canada. Their black hairless ears often are split from unacustomed frostbite. But they don't seem to mind.

The most remarkable thing about the 'possum—besides his odd appearance—which includes a pink nose, almost hairless white face, built-in grin, fat furry body, long hairless tail, and flat feet—is the fact that he is North America's only marsupial. Marsupials are pouched mammals like Australia's kangaroos. When young 'possums are born—about 18 at a time—they're so tiny that 20 would fit in a teaspoon. What's more, they're born blind, hairless and utterly helpless. The mother 'possum tucks them all into a built-in nursery pocket on her abdomen, where they stay warm and safe for two months until they're big enough to crawl out and hang on her back to go joyriding. The little ones clutch pawsful of hair and dangle from their mother's sides like tassels, bouncing against her ribs as she sways along.

'Possums will eat almost anything—as one fellow puts it, "from bats to blueberries." They raid people's garbage pails and gardens. In the woods, they poke after mice, toads, frogs, insects and will clean up anything another animal may leave behind.

A 'possum's hind feet are something special. His blunt big toe is "opposed," which means that it moves at right angles to the others—just like your own thumb moves in relation to your fingers. This enables him to grasp branches firmly. All his other toes—front and back—have strong claws for climbing. He uses his powerful tail like a monkey, wrapping it around limbs to anchor himself.

Footprints of a 'possum are easy to identify. His back feet make an impression similar to the hand of a human baby, while his front paws leave deep claw marks. And if the ground is soft, his long, powerful tail will leave a thin "drag" mark between the footprints.

HIND FOOT PRINT

OPOSSUM

Like the raccoon and the skunk, the 'possum can best be seen in a searchlight beam at night. And if you do spot one, you may be treated to some first class high jinks. One turned up in the headlight glare of my car recently. Instead of sensibly scuttling for the dark woods, this crazy fellow began racing in a tight circle. When I got out of the car, he saw me and "dropped dead." I picked him up by the tail, and he dangled like a wet dishrag. When I put him beside the road so that I could drive on, his mouth hung open and his tongue lolled in the dust. Then, as I turned and headed back toward the car, I heard a rustle behind me. I spun around in time to see the rear end of my "dead" 'possum scuttling up the bank and into the shrubs. He had faked death so perfectly that, even though I knew of this 'possum trick, I was thoroughly fooled by it.

Scientists have some evidence that when a 'possum does this, he has actually fainted. But the odd thing is that he always manages to revive from his faint at just the proper instant for a safe getaway. That's why many other people, including me, prefer to believe that the 'possum knows exactly what he's doing when he plays dead. Whether he does or doesn't, the animal's trick has earned him fame. Today the expression "playing 'possum" is used by Americans everywhere to describe someone who is faking stupidity or unconsciousness for a clever reason.

The Squirrel Family, like the Smiths and Joneses, has multiplied and spread to the far corners of the world. Today there are dozens of squirrel sub-families, sub-sub families, sub-sub-sub-families, and so on. You'll find members of their tribe in woods, fields, city parks, private backyards, and sometimes even in the attic—one place where we can do without them. The squirrel family name is "Sciuridae" (Sy-*ewe*-rih-dee), and includes familiar fellows like woodchucks, lemmings, gray squirrels, red squirrels, flying squirrels, fox squirrels and a host of others. In general, however, you could say that there are two main groups: Those living in the ground, and those living in trees. Since many squirrels are found only in certain localities, let's look at a few typical members of this big family who may turn up just about everywhere.

The woodchuck, or groundhog, and his larger cousin the Western hoary marmot, are ground dwellers well known to any farm boy or girl in this country. If you tramp across the fields or along the edge of the woods on a warm summer afternoon or evening, you may catch a glimpse of this roly-poly fellow—about the size of a fat, short-legged cat—waddling toward his den. Or perhaps he'll be squatting on his haunches on a rock, or rise of ground, munching away at a bit of stolen garden produce which he holds in his front paws, keeping an eye out for signs of danger.

WOODCHUCK HIND FOOT PRINT→

The best way to see a groundhog is to find his home, and to hide near its entrance at sunset. Finding this fellow's den is easy. Though occasionally he establishes himself in stone walls, most often he digs a big hole with an entrance six or eight inches wide. You'll recognize it by the pile of raw earth and pebbles around the entrance. Look for it on hillsides, in the woods bordering planted fields where the 'chuck can forage lazily for peas, lettuce, beans, corn and the other juicy vegetables he likes. Sometimes he'll have a hidden exit hole where he sits and warns his family of approaching danger with a piercing whistle.

Fat as they are, woodchucks can move with astounding speed when necessary. Many times I have watched one streak for the protection of the thickets in a confusion of running leaps and jumps, his plump sides jiggling like jelly. The tracks of a running 'chuck are confusing when you first see them, because he moves so energetically that his back feet pass his front ones with each leap. Hence, his hind footprints are always in front of his front paw marks like a rabbit's.

Gray Squirrels are among the sassiest of all the woodland animals you'll see on a daytime hike. The Eastern and Western gray squirrel and the red squirrel—all tree dwellers—blanket the country.

If other animals are scarce in your area, at least you can find a squirrel or see his tracks in the soft earth. His year-'round home is usually entered by a hole high in a hollow tree. But he also has a summer house plainly visible to an alert hiker. This dwelling is located in the highest branches, often in the same tree as the winter home. It is constructed of twigs, leaves, and bark, lined with a soft matting of grass, feathers, thistledown and the like. From the ground it looks like a ball of trash, similar to a crow's nest. The squirrel enters it from a hole in the side. In this breezy house, four or five babies are raised and taught the tricks of the squirrel trade. Watch the high branches for squirrels in late spring, and you may catch a glimpse of the young ones scampering along the limbs of the tree near the nest, mother or father perched nearby scolding them. You'll have to look sharply. The gray squirrel has a habit of scooting to the far side of a tree and flattening against the trunk to make himself invisible when danger is near. It is his protection against hawks and other enemies.

Gray squirrels don't store up great quantities of nuts like their chipmunk and red squirrel cousins. This is because they don't hibernate. However, you may see them busily burying nuts—one here and another there. Some experts think this is a waste of time, and that the squirrel never finds those nuts again. But no one is sure.

If you should find a squirrel in your animal trap, release him. He is an excitable fellow, and will break his teeth in desperate efforts to chew through the metal chicken wire of a cage or trap. To calm a trapped squirrel, just throw a dark blanket over the cage. For some reason, once he's in the dark, a squirrel feels safe and will promptly go to sleep.

GRAY SQUIRREL

HIND FOOT PRINT

RED SQUIRREL

The Red Squirrel is even more interesting to watch and study than his tamer cousin, so watch for him. He inhabits most of our timberlands, and his nests are like those of the gray squirrel. Nuts form his chief diet, but he also eats tender leaf buds, berries and even mushrooms. Somehow, he knows which mushrooms are poisonous, and avoids them. Mushrooms also spoil quickly, but this fellow knows it as well as we do, and gathers them at just the right time.

Since he hibernates in winter, the red squirrel spends a lot of time hoarding food during fall months. You can tell a busy hoarder by the size of his head. As he gathers nuts and grain, he tucks them in cheek pouches until his head swells three times its normal size. More than a bushel and a half of nuts have been found in the hollow tree nest of a pair of these squirrels. This storehouse—plus a few others nearby—were filled to tide the family over until the berries and seeds ripened again the following summer.

Don't look for a red squirrel's footprints near a stream. He seldom if ever drinks there. Instead, with his chisel-teeth, he makes a cuplike cut in the bark of a maple or birch tree and drinks the sap that collects in the cavity. If you search carefully, you may find half a dozen such squirrel "drinking fountains" on a single tree. We think we're pretty smart, tapping trees for maple sugar in the spring. But squirrels have been doing it for centuries.

The Cottontail Rabbit is a fellow who, sooner or later, will show himself to just about anyone who takes the trouble to watch for him anyplace in the country. You shouldn't have to go further than the nearest village green or your own back yard.

Before discussing the cottontail, there's a little confusion to straighten out about the Leporidae (Lee-*por*-ih-dee) family, which includes rabbits and hares. Most people have the idea that these two fellows are the same animal. They're not. But you can't always tell by their names. The snowshoe rabbit, whose popular name comes from the fact that his hind footprint resembles a miniature snowshoe, is not a rabbit at all. He's a hare. So is the jack rabbit, originally named "jackass rabbit" by Texas pioneers because of his extra long ears. To make things more mixed up, the pigmy hare is a rabbit, and so is the Belgian hare.

How these wrong names got started, no one knows. But they've stuck. Actually, it's easy to tell the difference between these two types of broadjump experts. Hares usually have long ears and long, powerful back legs. Rabbits, like the cottontail, have much shorter ears and stubby legs, and can't run nearly as far or as fast as hares. They scoot in swift zigzagging spurts from one hiding place to another. Both rabbits and

COTTONTAIL
RABBIT

HARE

HIND
FOOT →
PRINT

hares live in hollowed out nests, or "forms," hidden in low bushes, and lined with soft grass and hair plucked from their own bodies. Hares never have any other kind of nest, but rabbits frequently will take over abandoned burrows of other animals like woodchucks and gophers. Cottontails in Arizona sometimes are called "prairie dog" rabbits because so many have moved into old gopher diggings. Baby hares are born with a complete fur coat and wide open eyes, while newly born rabbits are hairless and have closed eyes for several days.

Everyone knows that rabbits are among the most timid creatures in the forest, but the odd thing is that they will grow accustomed to people quite readily. In neighborhoods where dogs are scarce, cottontails often burrow under the porches of houses and live there happily with footsteps pounding over their heads all day. If you set up a live animal trap in your yard, a rabbit will turn up in it sooner or later. A chunk of lettuce, celery, and tender, fresh peas-in-the-pod are good bait for him. In a cage he'll be fun to watch for a day or two, and will even lose some of his timidity. At first, he won't eat while you're watching, but will sit for hours, statue-like, staring straight ahead and twitching his pink nose.

Even though he seems to grow more tame with each passing day, a captured wild rabbit never stops trying to find some way to escape. And he may die of fright, or hunger if he refuses to eat. His normal life is about a year. And though some friends of mine have kept caged wild rabbits alive for more than four years, those people were animal experts. It's much better to let a wild rabbit go after you've had the fun of watching him for a few days.

2 Secrets in the Branches—and Under Them

When I was a youngster, a neighbor used to take us walking in the woods to find the striped maple tree. She'd pick several leaves, fold them into a purse for each of us, tuck a penny inside and fasten each stem securely through a flap cover formed by the leaf tip. That lady didn't intend to teach us anything special. But she did. Not one of us will ever forget what a striped maple tree looks like.

There are almost 2,000 different kinds of trees in North America alone. Even experts can't recognize all of them. But you'd be surprised at how many trees you'll be able to identify by learning to recognize their leaves. An interesting way to do this is by making leaf prints on sheets of paper that can be held together in a loose-leaf album. Identify and label each one as you print it. You'll soon recognize many of the trees that you pass on your hikes.

Before making any kind of leaf print, you need a leaf press to flatten and dry out the leaves you collect. This is easily done by slipping each leaf between the pages of an old magazine. With a dozen or so leaves inserted (don't stuff too many in at once, or they won't flatten), lay the magazine on a table and weight it down by stacking books on top of it. In a few days, your leaves will be ready for printing.

When you look for leaves to print, try to find perfect ones with interesting shapes. Picking a leaf or two from a tree will not hurt the tree. As long as about one-third of a tree's leaves are in place, they can do their job of making food for the tree.

Although there are many ways to make a permanent record of the leaves you collect, an album of leaf prints is undoubtedly the most fun.

To make a Paint Print you'll need water colors, a good brush, sheets of porous sketching paper (the pulpy kind you used to find in kiddies' crayon books is good), a smooth, round bottle and several sheets of plain white paper. Spread newspaper over your work table or desk. Choose the color you want and paint the veined surface of the leaf with it. Now place the leaf paint-side-down on the sketch paper. Do this quickly, before the paint dries. Lay a sheet of the plain paper over it and roll the bottle back and forth across the top sheet. Lift the top sheet and the leaf carefully (so as not to smudge the wet paint), and you'll find a perfect color reproduction of your leaf on the paper. Don't forget to label it promptly. If the print is incomplete, either the paint dried on the leaf or you didn't put enough on it. Be generous with the paint and wet your brush frequently.

Ink prints are made in much the same way. But instead of being brushed on the leaf, colored "printers" ink is spread on a piece of glass

with a rubber roller which then is rolled back and forth across the leaf until the leaf is well coated. The printing process is identical.

Spatter prints, which produce leaf silhouettes, can add interest and variety to your album. In this process, the leaf is pinned or tacked to the album paper. Then an old tooth brush is dipped into a thin mixture of poster paint, or colored pen ink. Point the brush, bristle side up, toward the leaf, and scrape the bristles toward you with a stick about six inches long. As you do this, the paint or ink will spatter the leaf and the paper. Keep spattering until you have a thick cluster of spots all around the borders of the leaf. Then carefully lift the leaf from the paper. Where it had been, you'll find a perfect outline of the leaf surrounded by an artistic shading of paint dots.

You can also make plaster casts of leaves—just the way animal tracks are cast. Only be sure to grease the leaf so it won't stick to the plaster.

The Woods Are Full Of Things To Collect or to photograph and study. Keep your eyes open every step of the way, and don't hurry. Usually it's a good idea to take along a pencil and notebook to record the animals you see, the birds nesting, and so on. When you go back that way next time, you can refer to your notes and observe any changes that have occurred. This is the way scientists work. A pair of binoculars and a camera can come in handy. The glasses will let you see things high in the branches that you might otherwise miss. And with the camera, you can take pictures of animal homes, birds' nests and other things that you won't want to disturb on summer hikes.

Look up in the high branches for signs of "arboreal," or tree animals like squirrels, opossums and raccoons. If you're lucky you may spot a huge round gray ball clinging to a branch. Don't disturb that, unless you're sure it's empty. But you may want a picture of it. It's the nest of the white-faced paper hornet—a big insect with a powerful sting. The nest is made of real paper, which the hornets manufacture themselves. They

do this by chewing wood pulp in their mandibles, or jaws, mixing it with water and with special juices made in their own bodies. This breaks down the tough cellulose, just as caustic soda or other strong chemicals are used to "digest" wood into pulp in paper mills. Each mouthful of this homemade pulp is carried by the hornets to the nest, then patted and shaped by their feet and mouths.

If you've heard an owl in your neighborhood, there's an easy way to find his tree. First, it will be a tree with a hollow in it somewhere. But the real clue to the owl will be lying on the ground around his particular hollow tree. When an owl eats a mouse, or a baby rabbit, he eats him bones and all. But the bones aren't digested. Instead they are rolled up in a tiny ball, and spat out. These are called "owl pellets," and you'll find dozens of them at the foot of every owl tree. It's a good idea not to disturb an owl. Even the tiny screech owl has been known to attack people in order to protect its young. An owl's nest is usually a sloppy collection of loose sticks, anyway. Contrary to popular stories, the owl isn't really wise —especially about his home. I know of one owl that laid three sets of eggs in succession on a sloping tin roof. The two eggs that didn't roll off and smash were thoroughly cooked by the sun-baked metal.

Collecting bird nests is interesting. But it should be done in winter when you're sure the owners have deserted them. Where do you look for bird nests?

Your own back yard is a good place to begin. Barn swallows may have built their homes of mud, grass and straw inside the family garage, up under the eaves. Wren's nests can often be found under the eaves of a house, firmly plastered with mud to the tiniest ledges or projections.

On hikes, you may be surprised at the odd nests you'll find on or near the ground. The little ovenbird, for instance, gets his name from the strange home he constructs on the forest floor. It is made of weeds and grasses, has a side entrance, and looks for all the world like a nest that fell from a tree and landed upside down. The bird's call, "teacher-teacher-teacher," is as curious as his home. Other ground-nesting birds with unusual homes are the bank swallows, who live in tiny hollowed-out caves in earth embankments; cliff swallows whose houses of mud pellets cling like clustered jugs to the sides of rocky walls; and chickadees, who dig their nests in rotten stumps. Many swamp birds live in ground nests among the reeds.

Check the heavy brush and thickets for nests of the thrush, robin, catbird, thrasher, and some warblers. This is the vireo's territory, too. He builds a unique nest that is always a three-cornered affair perched in the triangle formed by three branches. Look under bridges and on rocky walls for the phoebe's (*fee*-bees) cup-shaped nest of twigs, grass and moss.

Higher up in the trees, look for some of the oddest nests of all. This is where the Baltimore oriole, a master craftsman, hangs his carefully woven fabric of plant fibers, hair and odd bits of string. Some people leave strands of red yarn outdoors in springtime to help the orioles with their nest "knitting." The finished nest is a deep sack, suspended like a hammock from a sturdy branch. It is so strong that it will stay put for years.

A real find is a hummingbird's nest, but you'll have to look carefully to find one. It is no bigger than the bowl of a small pipe, made of bits of bark held together with spider web, and camouflaged with lichen. Usually it is perched on top of a limb in an orchard.

Getting to know the birds is a special hobby in itself. But if you make careful notes on the size and the plumage colors of those you see, it is easy to identify them in a good bird book. If you read carefully what the book says about them, you'll soon be able to recognize many by their calls—even though you may not see them. And you can encourage many birds to sing out for you if you have a handy little gadget called a "bird call."

You Can Make a Bird Call very easily. Here's how: Take a piece of close grained hardwood, such as rock maple or mountain ash, about two inches long and an inch square. A piece of an old hammer or axe handle will do nicely. You'll also need a screw eye that can be bought at any hardware store. Drill a hole slightly smaller than the screw threads in the end of the block, and turn the screw eye into it. Unscrew the eye, put a little resin powder in the hole, and screw the eye back in the hole. As you twist the screw eye back and forth in the hole, very slowly, you can make it chip, chirp, or trill in loud, clear, ringing notes. With practice, this simple device will produce an astounding variety of bird noises. And you'll be amazed at the number of birds that will answer your calls.

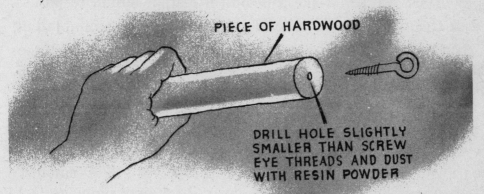

PIECE OF HARDWOOD

DRILL HOLE SLIGHTLY SMALLER THAN SCREW EYE THREADS AND DUST WITH RESIN POWDER

What makes this device work? The sounds are caused by the vibration of the wood as the tight screw is turned in it. The resin, being very dry, makes it vibrate even more. All sound, as you probably know, is caused by vibrations. Even a weighted string, swinging back and forth is vibrating and *making a noise*. But the vibrations are so slow you can't hear

45

them. Human ears begin to hear noise when something vibrates back and forth 16 times each second. Even then it is a very low tone. When the vibrations increase, we say the frequency is higher, and we hear it as a higher note. Tie a string tightly between two chair legs sometime, and pluck it. Tighten it more, and pluck it again. You'll soon get the idea. The bird call works on the same principle. If you turn the screw slowly, the vibrations will be slower, and the notes lower. The faster you turn it, the more vibrations you will produce each second, and the higher the chirps will be.

Things You Can Do With Feathers: Wherever you go on a nature hike, search the ground for the bright-colored castoff plumage of bluejays, robins, orioles and other birds. A collection of brilliant feathers, fastened to sheets of colored paper with transparent tape, will brighten the wall of any room. Or you can make a beautiful feather album by inserting the feathers you find in plastic envelopes and binding them in a looseleaf book. Until you're ready to mount them, they can be kept in plain envelopes which should be carefully marked. Any feather you find can be identified in a good bird book, and will help you remember the birds they have come from.

The best time to look for feathers is in late summer. That's when most birds molt, and begin to grow new plumage.

However, birds may lose some feathers almost anytime. Look in the thickets, where beating wings brush twigs in passing. Puddles and shallow pools, where birds bathe and preen themselves are also good places to search. There are three main kinds of feathers that a bird may have. The tiny, soft, fluffy ones designed to insulate him against heat or cold, are his down feathers. Slightly larger ones called "contour feathers" have heavier shafts and flat tips, but are downy at the base. These cover most of a bird's body and give him his general shape and color. The big, familiar flat feathers with a sturdy tapering shaft are the flight feathers found on a bird's wings and tail. The pointed, hollow end of a flight feather's shaft is called the "quill." The upper end of the shaft is filled with spongy material that makes it strong but flexible. This is the rachis (*ray*-kiss).

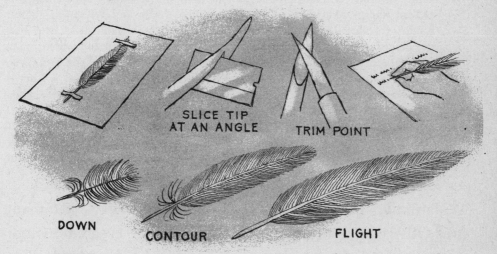

SLICE TIP AT AN ANGLE   TRIM POINT

DOWN   CONTOUR   FLIGHT

Making a Quill Pen: For years, people made excellent pens out of quill feathers. Many famous books of the Middle Ages were written with quill pens. All you need to produce one for yourself is a sharp razor blade. Slice the end of the quill diagonally from the underside, as shown in the accompanying sketch, sharpen the point, then make a short cut through the center of the point. One dip in an ink bottle will keep a quill pen like this writing for five minutes or more. For the best results use a large feather from a crow, hawk, chicken or turkey

An interesting thing about a feather is its color. Did you know there is no blue in a bluejay?

To prove it, all you need do is crush a bluejay feather in a bowl with a teaspoon, grinding it to fine particles. There won't be a speck of blue anywhere when you're finished. You'll only see dull gray.

This is because a bluejay's feathers have "structural" color, which means that the color is caused by refracted light. It is something like the kind of color produced by a prism. If you've never seen a prism, you can produce this kind of color yourself by placing a glass of water on a sunny windowsill and letting the bottom of the glass project slightly over the inner edge of the sill. On the floor, you'll see a whole rainbow of colors. The glass of water is a prism. A bluejay's "blue" comes to our eyes the same way—from millions of transparent, boxlike cells on the surface of the feather. Beneath them is a layer of dark gray cells. As light falls on the surface cells, it is broken up as it would be by the glass of water, and only the blue wave lengths of light are reflected back. Hence, to us, a bluejay looks very blue indeed.

The reasons why light and color behave this way are extremely complex. But if you have studied anything about light, you'll know that it consists of radiant energy, traveling in waves, just like radio and television signals. Each color is really a series of light waves that are longer or shorter than the others. A beam of white light is a combination of all the colors in the spectrum, or the rainbow that your glass made on the floor. You can prove this by taking a cardboard disc and dividing it into pie-shaped sectors of red, orange, green, blue, indigo and violet. Spear the center of the wheel with a pencil, spin the disc fast and see what happens!

When white light hits a prism, or a glass of water, or the transparent cells in a bluejay's feather, the different wave lengths of light are bent in different directions. The colors you see are the ones that are reflected back to your eyes.

Naturally, not all feathers are made this way, but many are. Others have ordinary "chemical" color, created by pigments in the cells which absorb some wave lengths of light and reflect only the others to us. These feathers, if ground up, will still have the same bright colors in the tiniest particles. The Oriole's brilliant orange is such a "chemical" color.

But whether colored structurally or chemically, feathers are fascinating things, and well worth collecting.

3 Exploring Streams and Ponds

Some of Nature's biggest surprises are hidden along the streams, ponds, and swamps that drain the country's wooded hillsides. Even the smallest trickle from a tiny spring is a menagerie of unusual wildlife. Along the muddy edges of the brooklet, where it gurgles through a shady ravine, dozens of red efts and salamanders wriggle in the cool dampness. In the woods surrounding the swamp, tiny tree frogs with suction cups on their feet cling to the trunks and branches of trees. In clear pools, mud puppies and colorfully striped minnows, like dace and rainbow darters, slither or dart in and out among the rocky crevices. Lift a stone from a quiet section of silty stream bottom here or there, and you'll find a delicate, semi-transparent crayfish—a perfect Lilliputian (Lil-ih-*pew*-shan) lobster. I have never seen a trickle in a rocky wooded gully that didn't hide some crayfish under its stones and boulders. The still water of swamps and ponds usually furnishes turtles, newts, tadpoles and an amazing variety of fresh-water fish.

Collecting stream and pond life, and building an aqua-terrarium (*ak*-wah-teh-*rehr*-ih-um) to hold what you catch, is a hobby that will prove endlessly rewarding. Any stream will do as long as it is not in a park or forest preserve where collecting is forbidden. Wear sneakers to wade in the brooks, so you won't slip or cut your feet on the rocky bottom. In swamps, heavy boots are a good precaution.

> *The Things You Need To Catch Specimens* and keep them safely are simple devices you can make yourself. Dip nets for scooping small, delicate animals from the water are a must. To make a small dip net, unbend a wire coathanger and form it into a loop about three inches in diameter. Twist the ends, as shown, to produce a handle about 14 inches long. With waxed string, stitch a sack of plastic or cloth netting around the loop ring, and you'll have a tool for scooping up specimens.
>
> A larger net is made the same way by increasing the size of the loop, and binding a piece of old broom handle to the stubby, twisted wire ends. It can be used to good advantage on larger specimens like frogs and fish in the ponds.

Plastic freezer boxes with tight tops in which you can punch a hole or two, make excellent specimen containers. A one-pint container will hold enough water to keep several specimens alive until you get home. Do not put salamanders, red efts or tree frogs in water. Many of them are land animals and may drown. Your aqua-terrarium should be all ready for the tenants before you start collecting.

Building An Aqua-Terrarium: A terrarium is just a large, glass-walled container like an aquarium, except that it doesn't have to be water tight. Instead of water, it contains layers of soil and gravel in which rocks, moss, small ferns and plants can be arranged to make a miniature habitat, or natural living place for small land animals. The only difference between this and an *aqua*-terrarium is the addition of a tiny pool, made by burying a shallow bowl or enameled pan in one end of the terrarium. The pool, two or three inches deep, will enable a few amphibious and shallow water creatures to be included in the miniature "jungle."

You can make an aqua-terrarium in a rectangular aquarium, if you have one. Otherwise, you can build a suitable tank yourself. A good size is about 18 inches long, as wide as a standard 12-inch plank "dressed," and a foot high. Here's what you'll need to make it:

1. Two pieces of glass the same size for side walls. (A hardware store can supply them or you can buy two cheap picture frames in the five and ten cent store and remove the glass from them. The glass should be as long as you want the terrarium to be and as wide as the tank will be high).
2. One-inch redwood or cedar plank, 12 inches wide and about four feet long.
3. Twelve feet of ½-inch quarter-round molding.

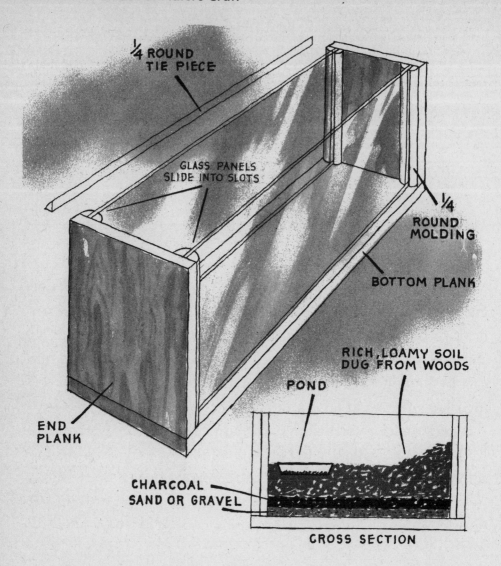

¼ ROUND TIE PIECE

GLASS PANELS SLIDE INTO SLOTS

¼ ROUND MOLDING

BOTTOM PLANK

END PLANK

RICH, LOAMY SOIL DUG FROM WOODS

POND

CHARCOAL SAND OR GRAVEL

CROSS SECTION

Cut a piece of the plank exactly as long as the glass, making sure the cut is straight and square. Now cut two more pieces, each one foot long. These are the end pieces which can be nailed or screwed (screws are better) to the bottom plank as shown. Cut eight pieces of molding in one-foot lengths and nail them to the inside edges of the end pieces as the diagram shows. Be sure to leave a space between each pair of strips just the thickness of the glass, so that the glass will slip easily into the slot. When this is done, you can slide the glass into place. All that remains is to place a strip of molding along the top of each side wall, and nail the strip ends to the edges of the end boards. This will make your tank rigid, and keep the end boards from bending outward when the terrarium is filled with earth and rocks.

When the tank is built, fill the bottom with a layer of sand or gravel about an inch deep. Don't use beach sand, because the salt in it will kill your plants. On top of this goes a similar layer of charcoal, for good drainage. Above this put a two-to-three inch layer of rich, loamy soil dug from the woods. When that's done, you're ready to build a miniature forest world. Shape the soil into hills and valleys, with a high and dry area at one end of the tank. Rocks and stones can be added to build little ledges and caves so the shy fellows have a dark, damp place to hide. At the low end, dig an excavation and install the "pond." A shallow black enameled baking dish about six or eight inches square is just about right. Cover the bottom with dark pebbles and fill it with water to a depth of about two inches. It is important that the pond have a dark bottom so the animals can see and recognize the water. Even in a watertight aquarium tank, the "pond" should be a separate unit so it is easily removed for cleaning and for freshening the water.

Plants For the Terrarium can be anything you want. The most effective are mosses, small ferns and low, leafy plants like violets and wintergreen with red berries. Use your plastic collecting boxes for plant specimens. Scout the cool, damp areas near a stream in a ravine. Perhaps you'll find star moss —a thick carpet of spongy dark green made up of what looks like myriads of miniature Christmas trees. In ledge-rock areas you may find decorative "caribou moss." The pale, bluish-green plant is a lichen (*lie*-ken), one of the earliest forms of life on this planet. Its crumbly coral-like structure resembles the branches of tiny leafless trees. In northern Canada, where it blankets the ground beneath the spruce trees from horizon to horizon, this primitive plant is the main diet of moose and caribou.

Around the rocks beside the shady stream look for dense mats of a shiny, dark green low-growing fern—the polypody (*pol*-ih-poh-dih). It's a thick, sturdy evergreen, excellent for a terrarium. In the higher woods, beneath hemlock or spruce trees in early summer, you'll find clusters of white or pink Indian pipes—a delicate plant shaped just like little clay pipes.

53

They will add a unique touch. A small jack-in-the-pulpit from a swamp wood makes a glamorous addition. In digging these things, make sure you get all the roots, then carefully plant them in the terrarium. They should be watered faithfully.

Catching The Terrarium's Population: Since a terrarium is small, the animals you put in it should be small—and not too numerous. The tiny amphibians and fish already mentioned are ideal inhabitants.

In this country, the most common salamander is the red spotted newt, and he's probably the one you'll find in your pond. Like all newts, he's an amphibian. He spends part of his life in the water, and part on land. Amphibians have been on the land longer than any other creatures, including reptiles —almost 350 million years, in fact. Their ancestors that first ventured from the water to make "amphibious landings" in the steamy beginnings of the world, probably were odd little fishes with stumpy legs. Of all amphibians today, salamanders are the most primitive. Even those living on land go to moist places or back to the water to breed. In some cases, salamander babies one quarter of an inch long are born alive. In others, 30 to 50 eggs are laid on an underwater leaf that is folded around them.

A few members of the family still spend their entire lives in the water. One such fellow is the mud puppy, whose gills branch out from behind his head like little trees. He lives in the quiet, mud-bottomed backwashes of lakes and streams. Look beside stones and sunken sticks for a small, brownish creature, from one to twelves inches long, with four perfectly formed legs and a slender tapering, finned tail. Scoop him up from behind with the dip net

To find a pale, white crayfish in a brooklet, look beneath stones on the bottom of the stream. These fellows vary from half an inch to two or three inches long in small streams. They are fast, too, so hold your net ready as you flip stones. In handling a crayfish, hold him by thumb and forefinger on either side of his body, otherwise he'll nip you with his little lobster-like claws. They don't really hurt but you'll feel the pinch, all right. He's another candidate for the terrarium pool. To make him happy there should be a mud bottom in the pool, some water plants and a rough stone under which he can hide.

The red eft won't be in the stream. He's a bright orange miniature creature about three inches long, with red spots. He crawls out from beneath stones and logs to wriggle along the forest floor after a spring or summer rain. He will be a red spotted newt—olive green with vivid reddish dots—in a few years, for he is the land phase of the newt's life. If you keep him alive in the terrarium, you may see him head for the pond one day to make his amazing transformation from land eft to water newt.

When you look for a red eft, under leaves and rocks in the woods above the swamp or pond, you may run into other cousins of his, such as the spotted salamander—a black shiny fellow with white spots—and the ringed salamander with stripes circling his body. Many people think, mistakenly, that these animals are "lizards." They aren't. Lizards are reptiles, and we'll get to them presently.

Your large dip net will come in handy when you begin scouting the pond and stagnant swamp water for small turtles, frogs and tadpoles. Polliwogs, of course, will grow into frogs or toads. In a well-balanced terrarium pool you can watch one grow legs and gradually lose his rudderlike tail. When he gets to be a full-fledged frog or toad, you'll probably have to let him go because he'll be too big for your zoo.

Around the edges of the swamp you'll find tiny tree frogs, about the size of a five cent piece. These are the "peepers" that serenade us with their chirping mating calls from early spring until late fall. They'll be found perched on stumps, and clinging to the trunks or branches of trees and bushes.

Once these animals are established in your terrarium, put the tank in a place that gets some sun part of the day. Cover it with wire screen, or a piece of glass raised a half inch from the terrarium top by small corks under the corners.

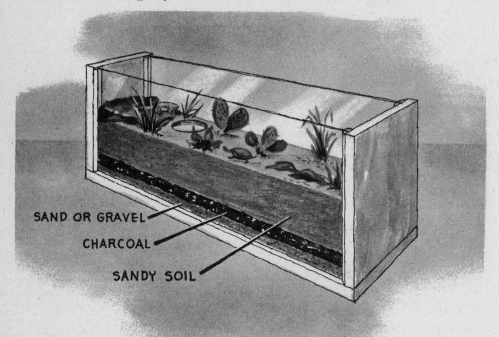

SAND OR GRAVEL

CHARCOAL

SANDY SOIL

The aqua-terrarium we have described here is especially suitable for plants and animals you'll find in moist, temperate areas of the country. It is just as possible to construct a desert garden in your tank to house dry climate creatures. The same base layers go in the tank, but use a sandier soil for the surface. And make sure there is a high, dry flat rock for the animals to sun themselves when they wish. Desert plants, such as small cacti, aloes (*al*-ohs), yuccas (*yuh*-kuhs), agaves (uh-*gay*-vees) and dry soil ferns provide interesting greenery. Rocks and driftwood will help the tenants to feel at home. A small saucer of drinking water is all the moisture required —though it is important to water the plants occasionally. Animals for this type of terrarium can include lizards, horned toads, snakes, land turtles, and the like. All these animals can be netted with a large, long-handled net.

What To Feed Terrarium Tenants:

Newts, salamanders, baby turtles, mud puppies, tadpoles, crayfish	Tiny bits of raw meat or fish Small worms Bits of raw oyster Chopped up scrambled egg
Frogs, toads, chameleons	Live flies, mealy bugs, meal worms
Minnows and fresh water fingerlings	Cracker and bread crumbs Small worms, commercial fish food
Box turtles	Earthworms, cooked meat, scraps, slugs, lettuce, apples, cabbage
Snakes and lizards	Live salamanders, toads, insects dangled in tank on a string (don't keep small amphibians in the same cage with these fellows)

Fun With Fishes: While you are scouting the streams and ponds, watch for the bright flash of darting minnows in the shadows of a rocky ledge. Many of these can be netted and installed in a home aquarium. Few people realize how many small bright colored fishes, just as interesting and beautiful as the more popular tropical fish, inhabit our native freshets, ponds and lakes. The rainbow darter, ablaze with red, orange, green and blue stripes, is a two-inch eye-stopper. So are many striped dace. The pale blue silverfin with black-edged side scales is another little beauty. He will play tag with his brothers in a bowl. Other quaint fish include the silvery "shiner," and the tiny redfin. One fellow, called the black-banded sunfish is an odd little black-striped fish with fins so transparent that he appears to move through the water by means of some mysterious invisible force. The little stickleback—a member of the carp family—will build a little basket shaped nest around the water plant stems in your aquarium. This unique, private underwater "cabana" is constructed with silky strands manufactured in special stickleback glands.

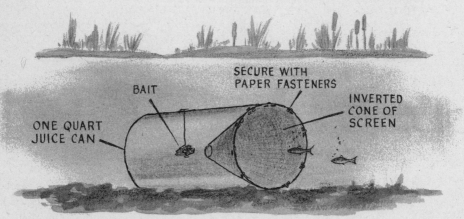

A large net is best for scooping up minnows. When a school of tiny fish swim by don't pass them up just because they look dull and drab from where you stand. Almost all fish have brownish-green backs to camouflage them from enemies. You can't tell from above what bright colors may flash from their sides and bellies. You can also construct a minnow trap, like the one shown in the diagram. If left for a day in shallow water near the reedy shore of a pond, it should yield a surprising catch.

Almost everyone knows how to create a balanced aquarium, and there are many books on tropical fish that will serve nicely for putting together a domestic fish tank. Here are just a few small tips that may be useful: Look for freshwater snails among the rocks and pebbles of the pond bottom. These little animals will help keep the bowl clean, eating the algae that forms, scavenging dead fish and other decayed matter. And when the snails come to the top of the water and stay there, it's time to change the water. Baby catfish, which you'll also find hugging the pond bottom, are good scavengers, too.

The study of fish and their habits is called "ichthyology" (ik-thee-*ahl*-oh-jee). It is a fascinating subject, for fish are strange creatures. Many eat their own babies and each other, but continue to exist because of the thousands of eggs each mother fish lays in great, jellylike masses. There's an interesting way to keep a permanent record of every type fish you catch. It is a method of making life-sized prints of the fish, that can be put in an album much the same as leaf prints.

How To Make A Fish Rubbing: Making an impression of a fish is an ancient Japanese art called "Gyotaku" (*G'yo*-tah-koo), and was used for many years in Japan by owners of fishing shops and seaside hotels to decorate walls. Gyotaku can be beautiful. Recently, ichthyologists discovered that these prints often show more clearly than photographs the delicate structure of a fish's scales and other features. As a result, a distinguished Japanese ichthyologist named Dr. Yoshio Hiyama, at the University of Tokyo, encouraged the art by writing articles about it and telling how it was done. Today, in Japan, a group called "Gyotaku-no-Kai," meaning "Friends of Fish Print," is busily turning out hundreds of fish rubbings. Just a few years ago an ichthyological artist, Mrs. Janet Canning, gave a demonstration of the art to officials at the American Museum of Natural History in New York City. Later the museum exhibited a large collection of fish rubbings from Japan in all colors of the rainbow. Here are Mrs. Canning's directions for making the beautiful prints:

1. Scrub the fish using a toothbrush and a solution of water and salt. This chemical mixture will dissolve the slippery mucous on his body. Soap or detergent will work, too.

2. Dry the fish with a damp sponge to get rid of any puddles around the gills and eyes. The fish should be damp, but not wet, or the paint will run and smear.

3. Stuff the gills with cotton (using tweezers) to prevent any water that may be under them from running out during the print-making.

4. Prop the fish with Plasticine clay to make his top surface as flat as possible. You'll get a better impression this way.

5. Fan the fins out, prop them with clay, and pin them through the clay onto the work board.

6. Paint the fins with glycerine so they won't absorb paint.

7. Keep an atomizer filled with water nearby, to spray the fish lightly now and then if he starts to dry out during preparations.

8. Apply the paint. Any good paint or printing ink can be used, in liquid form but not watery. Paint *with* the scales not against them. Paint around the eye.

9. Rice paper is best to use, but other fine absorbent paper will produce good effects. Silk or fine linen can be used. Hold one end of the paper on the work board behind the fish's tail, and tack it to the board. Don't let the paper touch the fish. Now, slowly press the paper against the fish with fingertips so an impression is made. When every part of the fish has been pressed against the paper, peel the paper away as you would lift a page in a book. Don't remove the tacks until you've studied the print. If there are weak spots, you can touch up that portion of the fish with fresh paint and lay the paper back. Then untack it, and peel the paper off.

10. Paint in the eye and the rubbing is complete.

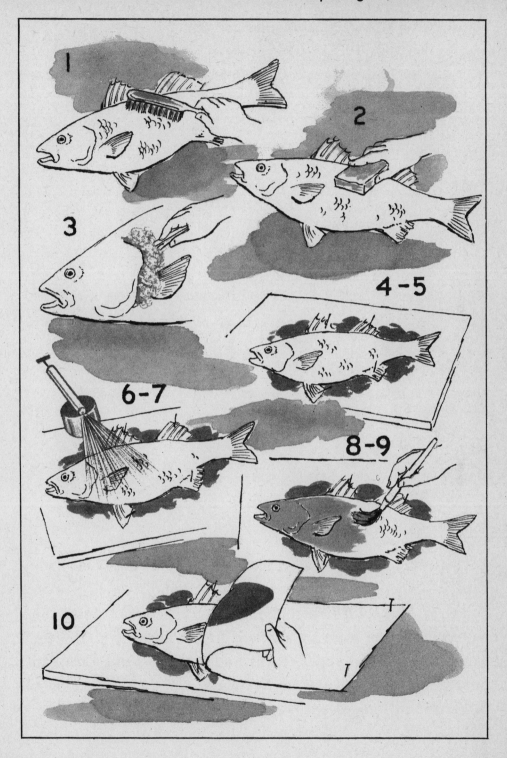

4 Across the Fields and Meadows

This chapter could just as well be called "Your Own Back Yard," "Down The Road," or "Look Around You Wherever You Are." The things we're going to collect, or poke into can be found in one form or another almost anywhere. Insects, wild flowers, plant seeds, rocks and soil are things we can turn around and see no matter where we stand—even on a city street in some cases. They're so common we hardly notice most of them. Yet, without them we'd have no world as we know it. By examining them closely and devising interesting projects or experiments with them, they'll soon come to assume the importance they deserve. Besides, things like insect collecting, flower and seed experiments and "rock-hounding" can be a lot of fun.

Making An Insectarium and filling it with a variety of local insects is an absorbing project that will enable you to see at first hand how these strange little creatures eat, lay their eggs and transform themselves in stages from grublike larvae to curious and often beautiful adulthood. The number of insects in the world is staggering. Entomologists, which is what the insect scientists are called, have discovered more than 625,-000 species so far and think there are hundreds of thousands more still to be discovered. If it weren't for the many natural enemies of insects, they might well run us off the face of the earth.

One of the first things to notice about insects is how they differ from mammals, reptiles, amphibians and fishes. They have no backbone. Their adult bodies often have on the *outside*, a shell-like skeleton made of "chitin" (*ky*-tin). The body is divided into three parts—head, thorax and abdomen. They have three pairs of legs and a pair of antennae, or feelers, which in some cases provide the insect with a sense of smell or touch. Adults usually have one or two pairs of wings. They breathe air through tiny tubes with openings in the body shell. Many insects have compound eyes. If you look at them under a magnifying glass, you'll see that they are made up of many little six-sided sections—each one a separate eye. An ant has about 50 little eyes in his two big ones. A dragonfly has thousands. Compound eyes are usually very large, taking up most of the head. Their roundness permits the insect to see in all directions at once.

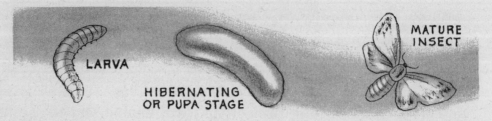

LARVA

HIBERNATING OR PUPA STAGE

MATURE INSECT

Insects have a curious life cycle. Some are born alive but most develop from eggs. What comes out of the egg is a squirmy little larva that people who don't know any better sometimes call "worms." When it is sufficiently fattened up, the larva goes into a sort of hibernating, or pupa, stage, during which the larva becomes a mature insect.

Where To Look For Insects: Crickets, grasshoppers, butterflies and a host of other interesting insects can be snared with a net in one single stroll across a meadow or empty lot. Have you ever wondered about the frothy little masses of white foam on the field weeds? It's made by the "spittle insect," or "froghopper." And the young bug is inside that foam, which he makes by squirting out a fluid and churning it up. No one is sure why he does this. Perhaps just to hide himself. He's a good prospect for study in an insectarium. Look under rotting logs or boards in the rank grass or shrubs at the edge of the woods where it's damp, and you'll find beetles. On the branches of fruit trees you may find the funny little treehopper, whose bright eyes, set far apart under a pair of quaint horns, are so designed that he appears to be wearing eye glasses. Climbing around the trunks and limbs of trees is where you'll find the walking stick, bearing such a close resemblance to a dead twig that he's easily missed. In spring, when fresh shoots are green, so is the walking stick. Later in the summer, when the new growth develops bark, the walking stick turns brown, too. Shady woods harbor the katydids whose noisy calls on July nights bring the forest alive with sounds. Most katydids look like pale green grasshoppers, and the males make all the noise. They do it by rubbing their outer wings together. This insect has been said to make more racket for its size than any living creature. Its call can be heard for a quarter of a mile on a quiet evening. Being caged up in an insectarium will not stop his song if he feels like singing.

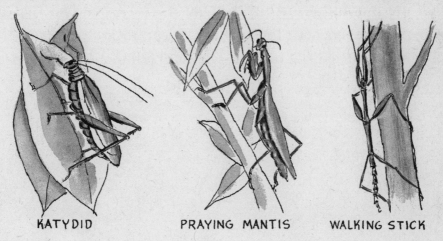

KATYDID   PRAYING MANTIS   WALKING STICK

Almost any shrub holds an army of small insects. If you spread a sheet beneath a bush and shake the branches, you'll have more insects in 30 seconds than you can identify.

A real find is a big praying mantis. He's a four-inch long fellow with a very big appetite. He gets his name from the pious way he holds his front legs. But don't let that fool you. He's not praying. His front legs are in just the right place to hold any other insect in sight, so that it can be eaten alive, on the spot. He is also the only insect we know about who can turn his head around and look back over his shoulder. A praying mantis may be found in almost any garden, if you're lucky. There's no telling where one may turn up. One flew into an office window on the 41st floor of the Empire State Building a few years ago. If you do find one, however, don't keep him in the same cage with other insects or you'll wind up with one insect—the mantis.

There are many interesting ways to catch live insects in traps. The night light diagrammed here, which you can easily make yourself, should bring you a grab bag of moth and bug surprises every time you set it out. A good beetle trap can be made by burying an empty tin can in the ground so that its open rim is even with the surface. Syrup or wet sugar in the bottom will attract the beetles, who will fall in and be trapped.

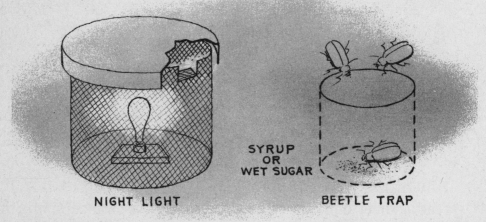

NIGHT LIGHT   SYRUP OR WET SUGAR   BEETLE TRAP

A good insect net can be made by bending a piece of coat-hanger wire around a big tree trunk to make the proper shape. Then remove it from the tree and wrap the loop ends firmly with string or wire to a three-foot piece of old broom or mop handle. A yard or so of mosquito netting is then sewn into the shape of a deep bag and laced to the wire loop. This device will serve for netting butterflies for collections, as well as live insects for the insectarium.

An Insect Cage can be anything from individual plastic or glass containers with holes punched in the top (for individual specimens) to large community cages for many bugs. You can make a big insect hotel from a cardboard carton. Cut windows in the sides and top, and cover them with screening or mosquito netting, fastened in place with brass paper fasteners. Cut a large three-sided flap door in one end, which can be lifted up to admit tenants or clean the cage. Newspaper can be put on the cage bottom to make cleaning easy. Pans of moist soil should be kept in the cage, along with two or three small potted plants. Cut flowers and tender shoots should be inserted daily to provide food for the leaf-eaters.

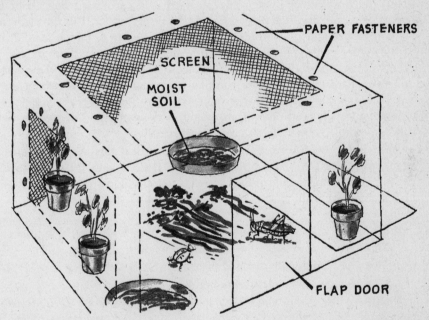

A cage like this will permit you to keep grubs, the larvae of bees, wasps and beetles, in the soil so they can develop. Keep them supplied with leaves from the tree on which you find them. Caterpillars eventually will spin their cocoons for the pupa stage on the plant stalks. Cocoons that you find in the woods should also be left attached to the twigs or stones on which they are found. Look for the pupae, or chrysalides (kri-*sal*-ih-dees), along the shady streams. They are often found inside the curled dead leaves of oaks and other trees whose brown foliage clings to the twigs after other trees have shed. Keep the insectarium soil moist but not wet, and don't put the cage where the sun will beat on it or the pupae inside the cocoons will dry out and die. Once a moth or butterfly has emerged, let it go. These delicate creatures will beat their wings apart in a cage.

A Grasshopper Greenhouse is fun to make, and will enable you to watch a few of these creatures, and perhaps a cricket or two as well, as they go about the business of living. All you need is a cardboard box about four inches deep, a baby food jar, and a quart preserving jar. Fill the baby food jar with water and place the box over it upside down. Punch a small hole in the center of the box and stick a few cut flower stems through it so the plants rise five or six inches above the box. Put the insects in the quart jar and turn it upside down over the plants so that the rim is resting on the box (see diagram). This arrangement will give the hoppers a homey environment, and will keep them from falling in the water and drowning. Plants should be replaced with fresh greens periodically.

Making An Ant Farm: Would you like to watch ants build a colony, lay eggs, talk by tapping each other with their feelers, and drill their amazing tunnels and passages in the soil? You can put a window on the private lives of the ants by installing some in an observation nest. Here's what you need to make one:

1. A piece of one-by-four-inch board, 12 inches long, for the base.
2. Three pieces of one-by-two-inch board, eight inches long.
3. Two pieces of ¼-inch plywood measuring 2½-by-10 inches.
4. Two pieces of glass measuring eight-by-10 inches.

Nail two of the eight-inch boards to the base board, in an upright position near each end, as shown in the diagram. The outside surfaces of the uprights should be just 10 inches apart. Place the two pieces of glass flat against the opposite sides of the uprights, and tape them in place with two bands of tape—one near the top, the other near the bottom. Tape the corners vertically. Nail the third eight-inch block flat against the plywood, centering it in the middle of the panel, as shown. This will be the lid, and should fit snugly over the top of the ant house. Fill the area between the glass panes with sandy soil, up to within about an inch and a half of the top.

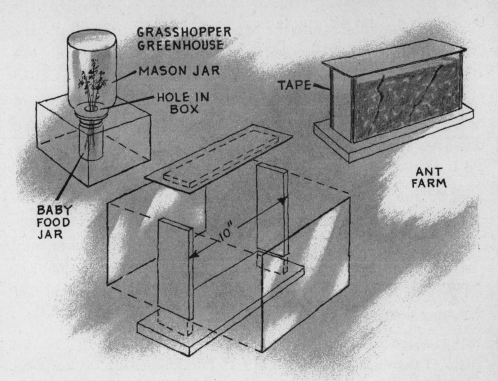

GRASSHOPPER
GREENHOUSE

MASON JAR

HOLE IN
BOX

TAPE

BABY
FOOD
JAR

10"

ANT
FARM

Now for the ant hunt! Bring along one of your plastic freezer boxes with a tight top for specimens; a long, light stick for picking them up; a trowel for digging them out, and a newspaper or old sheet. The best place to look for ants is under flat rocks and rotting logs. Black ants are best, usually, since many red varieties bite. When you find a nest, dig into it, spread out the dirt and start getting the ants to run up a stick —then brush them off on your newspaper or sheet. When you have collected 50 or so, pick up 20 or 30 of the little white eggs and grubs, too. In order for the colony to function well, it is important to have the queen. To find her, dig deeply into the center of the nest, dump each trowel load on the spread-out newspaper or sheet, and crumble the lumps of earth. Watch carefully for an ant that will be much bigger than the others. That will be the queen.

Dump your catch into the top of the ant house, and put the lid in place. An occasional sprinkle of water from an eye dropper will keep the soil properly moist. A bottlecap filled with a solution of sugar and water will provide plenty of food. Cake crumbs and canned fruit syrup will be welcomed occasionally. If you want to see some action, drop a strange ant, a live fly or a spider into the nest now and then.

The ants will drill tunnels through the soil and along the inside of the glass where you can watch them store the eggs and care for them. If you're lucky, the queen's chamber may be excavated where you can see it and watch her lay the eggs of a new colony. Ants don't like daylight, so cover the nest when you're not watching it.

Feeding List For Live Insects:

1. Grasshopper, walking-sticks	Fresh grasses and weeds. Clumps of sod in the cage, watered occasionally will last several days. Put soil in the cage for them.
2. Beetles	Grubs, caterpillars, meal worms. A piece of rotten wood with soft insects in it will keep a beetle happy. Give him a tin of water, too.
3. Crickets	Wet bread chunks, lettuce, peanut butter. Give them water, and soil to dig in.
4. Caterpillars, tree hoppers	Leaves from the plant on which they are found. Lettuce leaves. When they start spinning a cocoon, they won't need anything.
5. Praying Mantis	Small live insects, gathered by shaking a bush over newspaper. Bits of raw chopped meat.

Mounting Butterflies and Other Insects by putting them to sleep in "killing jars," then installing and labelling them in permanent cases, is a good way to learn the names of many varieties so that you'll be able to recognize them in the field. An insect guide book will not only help you identify the specimens, but will tell you many interesting things about them.

Equipment you'll need for collecting and mounting includes a net (the one described for snaring insect zoo tenants is just right); killing bottles (mayonnaise jars with tops will do); carbon tetrachloride (tet-rah-*kloh*-ride); envelopes for carrying specimens home; wood blocks for making a spreading board (see diagram); straight pins and paper strips for spreading wings; jars and cigar boxes for mounting specimens; gummed tags for making labels.

When you set out, take net, tweezers, carbon tetrachloride, a wad of cotton, envelopes, and a killing jar with you into the field. Most of the equipment can be carried in a canvas bag with shoulder strap.

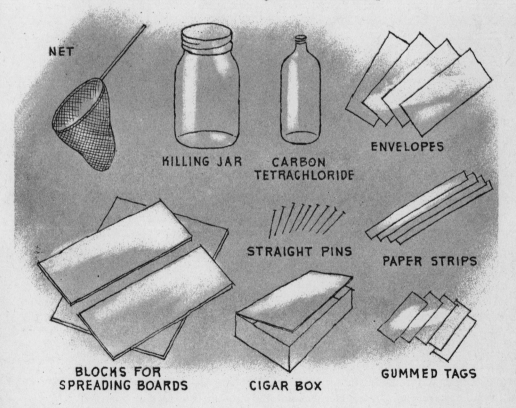

NET

KILLING JAR   CARBON TETRACHLORIDE

ENVELOPES

STRAIGHT PINS

PAPER STRIPS

BLOCKS FOR SPREADING BOARDS   CIGAR BOX   GUMMED TAGS

Carbon tetrachloride is a dry-cleaning fluid and gives off fumes that can be damaging to a person's liver if too much is inhaled. So be careful with it. There is no danger if you use it outdoors in the fresh air and don't breathe more than a few whiffs at a time.

To prepare your killing jar, wad some cotton in the bottom, soak it with the carbon tetrachloride and put another cotton wad over this so the liquid won't damage delicate wings. A good way to get the insect into the jar is to put the jar into the net, work the specimen into it, then clap the lid in place. The specimen will stop moving in about three minutes, but should be left for 15 minutes. Take him out gently, slip him in an envelope and look for the next subject.

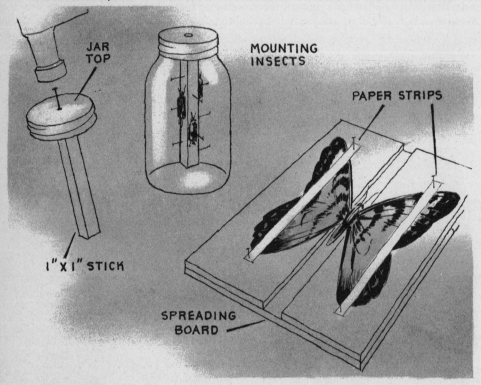

Back home, if the butterflies and moths have folded their wings and are stiff, you can soften them by leaving them in a jar with a water-moistened blotter overnight. As soon as possible, spread them on the spreading board so their bodies fit in the groove, and pin thin paper strips vertically across the wings. Do a wing at a time, handling the bugs gently with tweezers to avoid damaging them. In a day or two, they'll be dry and ready to mount in the bottom of a cigar box. Mounting pins should pierce the center of the thorax. Don't forget to stick a label beneath each mounted specimen after you've identified it in your insect book.

Smaller insects can be effectively mounted around the sides of one-inch-square sticks about four inches long. Nail the top end of the stick to the inside of a metal jar top, nicely centered. Then screw the cap on the jar. You can have any number of permanent glass-enclosed exhibition cases by using this simple system.

Tricks With Flowers, Plants, And Seeds: Nearly everyone has seen unusual or especially pretty wildflowers, picked them, brought them home and stuck them between the leaves of a flower book until he finds time to look them up. That's where the blossoms usually stay until someone else opens the book and the well-pressed bloom, brown with age, falls out and crumbles on the floor. This is too bad, because a lot can be learned by studying blossoms. And it's possible to press flowers so that they will retain their color and last for many years. We'll get to that shortly.

First of all, flowers shouldn't be collected willy-nilly. It's a wise idea to hunt only for those in your own area as a starter. Be sure to pick one or two from large clumps, so that some will be left to multiply. When you hunt for them take a good sharp knife to cut stems cleanly and a shoe box for carrying the cuttings. Line the box with waxed paper and fill the bottom with damp moss or wads of wet cotton to keep the flowers fresh. Look for perfect blossoms with even, bright-colored petals and with delicate center structure intact.

Perhaps you've noticed the fat seed pods atop the stalks of flower plants. If you break one open sometime, you'll find it chock full of nearly ripened seeds. Some people collect seeds as well as flowers because of their distinctive, and often curious, features. Since plants can't walk around and put their seed offspring in new, fertile soil where they'll sprout and grow properly, Nature has provided them in many cases with seeds that can travel.

Dandelions, thistles, willow trees and cotton plants grow tiny round seeds with huge feathery tops. When the pods open, the seeds float away on the air and are carried far and wide by summer breezes. Flowers of fruit trees hide their seeds inside a sweet juicy casing that many animals like to eat. So, animals spread the seeds. Everytime you eat a picnic peach or plum and throw the pit across the fence, you are planting a seed for some fruit tree.

Some shrubs grow hooklike barbs on their seeds. When an animal brushes against them, the barbs cling to his fur and the burr seeds go for a long, free ride.

It doesn't take much encouragement for some seeds to sprout and start growing. You can watch this process yourself by setting up a simple experiment. Collect a handful of fast-sprouting seeds that are easy to find—lima beans or corn kernels are good. Curl a piece of blotting paper around the inside of a tumbler, moisten it, and slip the seeds in between the blotter and the glass. Put the glass in a warm place. Keep the blotter moist for several days and watch what happens.

You can see for yourself how any plant will actually *move* itself under certain conditions. To see how gravity affects a plant's roots, take a bean that has just begun to sprout (one of those from your blotter tumbler will do), and spear it lengthwise with a long pin. Stick the end of the pin in the bottom of a cork. Now take a bottle, stuff a little wet cotton in it, and insert the bean in the bottle until the cork is firmly seated in the neck of the bottle. Turn the sprouts upward, put the bottle in a dark closet and check it every hour or so to see what those sprouts are doing!

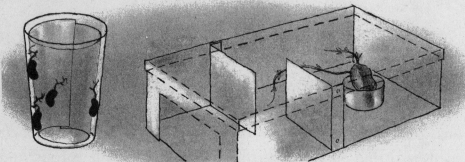

Light has a powerful effect on plants. You can test this by putting two tabs inside an old shoebox, just as they are in the diagram. Cut a hole in one end of the box, then take a fast growing plant, such as a potato with sprouting eyes, and set it in a cup of water at the end of the box opposite the hole. Cover the box and point the hole at a window. Watch what happens to the shoots growing from the potato by checking every few days. Then leave the cover off and see what happens.

Of all its living parts, the flower is one of the most important things to any plant. Without it, plants could not reproduce themselves. That's one reason why it is fun to collect and study flowers. To preserve all the delicate parts of a blossom, care should be taken in pressing it.

You Can Make A First Rate Flower Press with nothing more than a stack of tabloid newspapers; two sheets of plywood the same size as the papers; a dozen sheets of corrugated cardboard cut from grocery cartons—also the same size as the papers; a pair of leather straps with self-tightening buckles.

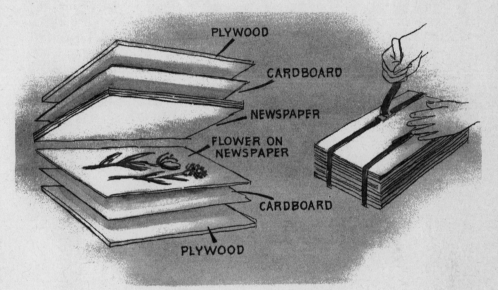

First, lay down a plywood board. On top of this put a cardboard panel. Next come two double sheets of newspaper, folded. On this, lay out several small flowers or one or two big ones. Four more newspaper pages go on top of them. Then, more specimens, and so on. Add another cardboard at every fourth or fifth layer, cap the top with the other piece of plywood, and bind the pile tightly together with the straps running lengthwise. Keep the press in a dry place. Plants are ready to remove when they are thoroughly dry, but not brittle.

Pressed flowers may be kept in a scrapbook, labeled with their names, date and place found, and any other particulars desired. Or they can be framed. Some people arrange them artistically under glass-topped trays, along with butterflies they have collected. Beautiful screens can be made by arranging pressed flowers, leaves, ferns and butterflies between two big sheets of fiberglas plastic, fastened together with plastic cement and set in wooden frames. If properly pressed, plants used in this way will keep their color for many years.

Who hasn't scaled a flaky piece of shale across a pond to watch it skip?—or pitched a rock at a tree? But did you ever stop to think, when you did it, that this stone was a piece of the earth's foundation? Our whole planet is nothing more than a great ball-shaped rock, molten in the center, with a hard, wrinkled, broken and well-worn crusty shell on the outside.

How The Rocks Were Formed: About five billion years ago, the earth, still red with the heat of its own internal fires, hurtled along its orbit through the thin clouds of matter from which it had formed.

In the cold darkness of space, the hot liquid surface began to "freeze" solid, or crystallize, as its temperature dropped below 2,000° F., which is about the highest melting point of rock. For thousands of years, great volcanic explosions ripped through the thin, newly formed crust, still glowing with heat, and spewed fresh seas of molten lava across the surface. As deeper layers of the crust solidified and shrank, the outer surface heaved up in great wrinkles—just the way the skin of an apple wrinkles when the inside begins to dry out. Vast stretches of the crust broke, folded over itself, and heaved massive edges skyward to form mountains. Overhead, a solid blanket of black clouds blotted the sun from the glowing face of the new planet. Water vapor that started to condense into rain drops high in the frost of space, evaporated the instant it fell into the scorching atmosphere—and was sent soaring upward again without touching the ground.

Finally, one day the rain fell and did not sizzle away, for the rocks of the new crust had thickened and cooled below the boiling point of water. Then, for hundreds and hundreds of years, rain fell without stopping. Great deluges of it poured in cataracts down the volcanic ridges and slopes. It carried huge chunks of new rock from the peaks and tumbled them crashing into the valleys. The rocks shattered and rubbed against each other in churning rivers that ground them to powder. The rivers washed the powder and rock crumbs to the bottom of newly formed seas and, in the seas, life was born.

But still the earth did not stop rumbling. The imprisoned forces beneath the crust heaved the sea bottoms upward, and the mountains slumped into the sea. Primitive plants grew in the sea-bottom silt that now stood on plains above the water. The plants added their particles to it as they died and rotted away. Volcanoes still spewed their lava through newly formed cracks in the crust and lifted mighty chunks of it that squeezed and twisted the layers under tons of pressure and heat, giving the old rock strange new forms. Glaciers grew and carved new valleys and plains as they ground slowly across the earth's face.

For millions upon millions of years, the rains, seas, volcanoes and glaciers have continued to carve up our planet's crust. The process is still going on.

In the layers of different colored rock in the cliff walls of our great canyons; in the glassy, spongy or hard black rock of volcanoes; in the odd-shaped stones of boulder-strewn valleys; in the glittering mineral particles in the soil of the valleys and sands of the beaches; and in the glinting crystals of stone and metal buried under the hard face of mountains—the secret of our world's creation and history lies hidden. That is why "rock-hounding" and the study of mineralogy is of great interest to us.

> *How Soil Can Come From Rocks:* It's hard to realize how the hard, volcanic lava and other fire-formed rocks, which were part of the earth's beginning can have produced the deep, fertile soil in which our forests and vegetable foods grow. There are some interesting things you can do to see how this happened. Ordinary glass, which is similar to volcanic rock, can be used as a substitute in this experiment. Heat the glass on a cookie tin in the oven until it is good and hot. Then dump it quickly into an old pot of ice cold water. What happened to that glass is the same thing that might have happened to the hot rocks of the baby world as the first rains hit it.

The reason glass and stone shatter this way is because sudden cooling shrinks together the molecules of the outer surface much faster than those inside, setting up such strong stresses and strains in the material that something must break. In New Zealand, where engineers were drilling into a volcanic valley for natural steam, I have watched red hot rocks from deep in the crust, shoot from the drill holes and explode in the air like bombs due to the sudden temperature change. Soil is also made by rocks weathering away in other ways, such as pounding together in streams. Rub two soft stones together and see the pile of soil that results.

To see how closely some parts of real soil resemble what you've made with bottle and stones, take several sturdy sandwich bags or empty salt sacks for soil sample bags, and collect a few soil specimens from different places. First examine your specimens under a magnifying glass, and notice the different size bits and pieces. Then empty each pile into a separate glass of water and let it settle. On the bottom will be the coarse chunks of shattered rock crystals broken from the parent stone. Graded upward will be finer and finer particles of ground rock, with the finest sediments, ground to powder by glaciers and weathering, on top, along with decomposed bits of living things.

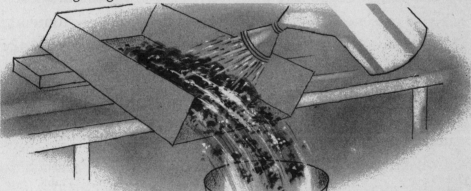

This is the way soil is deposited in the sea bottom, carried there by rivers and streams. You can see how rivers do this by filling a shoe box with fine soil and tearing off one end. Tilt the box by putting a small block of wood under the closed end, and let the front end project off the edge of a table. Put a bucket on the floor to catch the run-off, and spray the soil several times with a watering can. Check the bottom of the bucket, and you'll find sediments. Observe what the running water did to your "land" in the box. Water, running down hills for centuries can carve great valleys just like the little one in your shoe box. It shapes the land in other ways, too. If you fill a pan with loose soil, keeping it level, and sprinkle it gently, you'll see how raindrops can create "mesas" and other odd land forms.

Kinds of Rocks and How They Grew: Great but gradual movement of earth's crust along with weathering, have buried vast layers of sands, muds, clays and other sediments; compressed and often cemented, they have turned into the sedimentary rocks, such as shale, limestone, and sandstone.

The hard, tough rock formed from the molten material of the earth when it cools is called igneous (*ig*-nee-us) rock. Granite, and a blackish rock called basalt (ba-*solt*), and the pumice (*pum*-iss) and glassy obsidian found near volcanoes, are igneous. Then there is a third group of rocks that once were sedimentary or igneous, but have been changed by great heat and pressures during mountain-building eras. These are called metamorphic (met-a-*mor*-fick) rocks and include such things as schist, which once was shale or slate, and gneiss (nice) which can start life as granite or even a sedimentary rock.

The reason these rocks are so different from sedimentary ones is due to the way they were formed. When a molten substance cools and solidifies, a strange thing happens to the atoms and molecules of which it is made: they line up in special patterns according to their chemical combinations. As more and more of them gather together, they build little clusters of themselves which we call "crystals," with straight-sided shapes so regular and smooth that they look as though a jeweler cut them. Most igneous rocks are made entirely of crystals.

Make A Crystal Garden, and you can see how crystals form. You won't need heat and pressure, because some crystals form chemically and that's the kind you'll make. Here's what it takes: pieces of brick or coke or coal—about the size of golf balls; a glass or china bowl to put them in; ammonia; rock salt or common table salt; liquid bluing; a tin can for mixing things; a mixing paddle or spoon; water.

Put the chunks of brick or coal or coke (you can put them all together if you like) in the bowl until it is about half full. In the mixing tin pour a quarter of a cup of salt, a quarter of a cup of bluing, a quarter of a cup of water, and one tablespoon of ammonia. Mix it well and pour this slowly over the chunks in the bowl. Almost immediately you will see little crystals start forming. In two or three hours, your brick and coke will have sprouted a forest of fantastic crystal shapes.

You can color your crystals too. Color tablets used for dyeing Easter Eggs are very inexpensive. Dissolve one tablet of each color into 1 tablespoon of water. Mix thoroughly. Then, after your coal is saturated with the salt mixture, pour the coloring drop by drop with an eyedropper.

CHUNKS OF COKE AND BRICK

AMMONIA BLUING ROCK SALT

Rock crystals form in much the same way, separating themselves into groups of crystalline substances. Metals, such as iron, copper, silver and gold are crystalline. So are a host of other things like quartz, flint and precious stones.

Over the years, man has found many uses for the crystalline substances in rock. First he chipped flinty stones for weapons and tools; later he found metals, like iron, and discovered that by striking these two things together he could make fire.

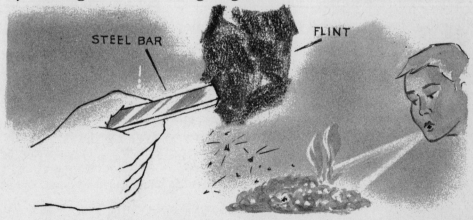

STEEL BAR

FLINT

You can try this yourself with a small piece of flint and a steel bar. On a wad of cotton, sprinkle a little pile of wood powder, tinder or fine dry saw-dust. Then hold the flint in your left hand and strike it sharply with the iron or steel bar. Little sparks will fly from the flint. Try to aim these at the sawdust. When a spark hits the pile, blow it quickly so the sawdust begins to smoulder. As you blow, feed strands of cotton into the glowing dust until it catches fire. And there you are. It isn't easy, but can be done with practice. After all, primitive man for centuries had no other way to make fire and supply himself with heat—the basis of all his useful energy.

The Heat And Energy In A Stone: It is odd to think that heat and energy can be locked up in a cold stone or a piece of metal, but they are. What causes a flint to throw off little white-hot sparks when you hit it? The sudden friction of the bar against the stone raises the temperature of a tiny speck of the flint just the way friction with the atmosphere makes a meteor or a *sputnik* glow as it plunges to earth. From the heat of the flint's spark the sawdust begins to oxidize, or decompose, just the way iron oxidizes and grows rusty—only much faster. When this happens, oxygen in the air combines with gases given off by the smouldering sawdust, and *fire,* or combustion is the result.

Getting To Know The Rocks and what they mean to us can can be a deeply absorbing pastime. Because there are so many rocks, most people limit themselves to certain types of col-lecting. For any kind of mineral collecting, or rock-hounding, however, you should have some special equipment:

1. A good hammer to break specimens to walnut size for storing.
2. A small cold chisel for splitting rock seams open.
3. Sturdy egg boxes or plastic partitioned trays to keep specimens orderly.
4. A magnifying glass to see crystal structure in rocks.
5. A canvas bag with shoulder strap for carrying rocks home.
6. A piece of unglazed white tile for scratch tests. Many minerals can be identified by the kind and color of mark they make on such a tile. A rock collecting book will tell you which minerals make what marks.

Here are a few special types of rock hounding:

Crystals—Many of these are common and fun to collect,

like beautifully colored quartz, easy-to-find semi-precious stones like garnets, and interesting metallic crystals like the little square crystals of pyrite, or "fool's gold." Other interesting crystals of ore are buried in many igneous rocks. Stream beds are a good place to look for all of these. So are the dumps around mines and quarries, if you can get permission to hunt there.

Fossils—These are the impressions of plants and animals that fell into the soft sediments in river deltas, and in lake and sea bottoms. More sediments covered them. Then the sediments were solidified, and the marks left by the primitive living things were sealed forever inside the rock.

To see how this happens, coat a leaf with vaseline and lay it on a flattened piece of modeling clay about the size of a pancake. Then, take another clay pancake and lay it on the leaf. Press it down hard with the heel of your hand, applying pressure over the whole surface. Now, pull the clay patties apart, remove the leaf, and you will see an artificial "fossil" leaf imbedded in each piece of clay.

Look for real fossils along the shores of old lakes, and in

sharply cut banks of streams where sandstone, limestone, and shale layers show clearly. People who collect fossils often look also for the tools that primitive people carved from stone—flint arrowheads, stone axes and knives are often found in the same places with fossils, and give us an interesting peek at the customs of our forefathers.

Fluorescent Minerals—Some dull-looking crystals will blaze a fiery red, green, blue, orange or other startling color if something called "black light" is flashed on them. Black light is invisible ultra-violet light. Remember the rainbow spectrum produced by the glass prism in the bird chapter? Well, ultra-violet light comes right next to the violet band that you saw on the floor. But its wavelengths are too short to be seen by human eyes. Besides, few ultra-violet rays from the sun's light penetrate the earth's atmosphere. But by producing them with a special mercury or argon lamp—available in most electrical shops—these invisible rays will cause the electrons in some mineral crystals to move around excitedly, releasing energy in the form of visible light. Many people have made a unique and enjoyable scientific project of collecting fluorescent minerals and setting them up in displays under ultra-violet light tubes. Fluorescent minerals may be found almost anywhere, but mine dumps are the best place to look.

The riches of Nature are found everywhere, but no place is her bounty as plentiful as it is in the restless seas, along their tidal ramparts and on their sweeping beaches.

Life swarms on the pebbled, sandy, and coral-gardened floor of the continental shelves off our coasts. Creatures encased in rainbow-colored shells tunnel through the wet sand and mud. Myriad living things, modeled in every shape and color, drift through the blue-green depths in a dim, watery world of strange lights, noises and floating forests of seaweed. Nowhere else in the world we know has Nature let herself go with such abandon in the business of creation. Creatures trail great living draperies behind them, headlights flash from their eyes, some are shaped like sunbursts; others like bells. Some crawl, some swim, some move through the depths by jet propulsion.

And in the water of the sea itself a hoard of precious things are locked—metals such as gold, and a wealth of other minerals. Sea water itself is an endless storehouse of nuclear energy, once scientists find a way to release it.

Take a good look at it. It is pretty important to this planet. It covers three-quarters of the earth's surface. If the earth were a smooth, round ball without continents and mountains, there would be enough water to cover the entire globe 8,000 feet deep!

Sea water is a combination of gases and solids. You can see the solids in it just by putting a pot of sea water on the stove and boiling it until all the water is gone. The bottom of the pot will be covered with crumbly white material. Three-quarters of this is salt. Taste it. The rest is a combination of almost every element we know. How did these solids get in the sea? Rain water on the land has been dissolving them from the rocks and soil, and carrying them to the seas for billions of years.

Like all liquids, water has many curious properties. One of the most interesting and useful is its buoyancy, which permits us to sail ships on it, and to swim in it. Why does a stone sink and a block of wood float? The reason is that the block of wood weighs less than an amount of water the same size and shape as the block. We say that the "density" of the wood is less than that of water. Such a block of wood—or anything—will sink down only until it has "displaced" an amount of water equal to its own weight. Then it stops sinking. Most rocks, for their size, weigh much more than an equal volume of water. So they sink.

Not all wood has the same density. Try to find two wood blocks of the same size—one of pine, the other of mahogany. Put them both in a pan of water and look at the difference in how they float.

Because of the many heavy minerals dissolved in sea water, it has a greater density than fresh water. That is why it is easier to swim in the ocean, and why ships can be more heavily loaded when they sail in sea water than when they sail in fresh water. Drop a fresh egg in a glass of salt water; then do the same in fresh water and watch what happens.

PIN

SALT WATER   FRESH WATER

Another curious thing about water is that, like all liquids, it has a thin, invisible film drawn tightly across its surface. It is called "surface tension." Because of this strange phenomenon, small things of greater density than water often can be made to sit on top of the water. For instance, you can float a pin in a glass of water if you do it carefully. Be sure the pin is thoroughly dry. Place it crossways on the tines of a fork, and gently lower the tines into the water until the pin "floats" off. Notice how the water surface "bends" under the pin. That is surface tension.

Shells And Beached Creatures Tell About Sea Life: Few people can afford to hire ships and go to sea to study the oceans and the life in them. But you can learn a great deal about life in the oceans by "beach combing" for shells, and strange creatures washed up on the sands by tides.

Besides introducing you to hundreds of sea curiosities, a shell collection is beautiful and decorative. Most shells are made by creatures called mollusks. The material in them— mostly lime—is taken from the sea water and manufactured into shell material for a portable house by the mollusk himself. It's doubtful that you'll ever collect all the kinds of shells there are, because there are 75,000 different species of mollusks known—and perhaps many still unknown.

There are two main kinds of shells to look for—univalves, which come in one piece, and bivalves, which come in two halves and are usually hinged in the middle like oyster and clam shells.

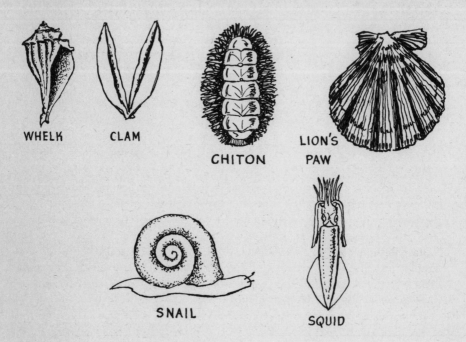

WHELK   CLAM   CHITON   LION'S PAW

SNAIL   SQUID

Only five main types of sea animals make shells. A sluggish fellow called the chiton (*ky*-ton) is one. A chiton shell has eight little shells along its back, overlapping each other like shingles on a roof.

A longish mollusk, called the scaphopoda (skah-*fop*-oh-dah), with little tentacles on his front end, makes a univalve shell shaped like a miniature elephant tusk. They are called "tusk shells" and usually are long and tapered.

Clams, oysters and mussels make the bivalve shells with which we are all so familiar.

The snails make a wide variety of often beautiful shells in the shape of a coil.

Squids make the fifth group of shells. They are called cephalopods (*sef*-uh-loh-pods)—which means "head-footed." Many of them, like the octopus, have no shell at all. Argonauts and the nautilus are cephalopods which make large, delicately colored shells that spiral. An odd thing about the argonaut's shell is that it is not attached to the animal's body. It is made only by the female argonaut who carries it with her to hold her eggs.

The best time to hunt for shells is right after a storm, along a section of beach where swift ocean currents wash the shore. While you're hunting for rainbow-hued shells, don't overlook the little domelike shell structures of sea urchins, and flat round sand dollars with quaint raised patterns, made by an urchin with little black spines on his back.

Starfish, from little two-inch fellows to the 12-inch giant star, add great interest to a shell collection when dried in the sun. Little ones can be painted and used as curious Christmas tree ornaments. Sea urchins, sand dollars, and starfish belong to another group of animals called Echinoderms.

Shells, like other collector's items, should be identified, labeled, and stored in cabinets or partitioned trays. But there are other interesting things you can do with shells. Tiny ones, with holes drilled through them, can be strung into jewelry like necklaces and bracelets. Shells can also be stuck to cigar box tops in clever patterns with plastic cement.

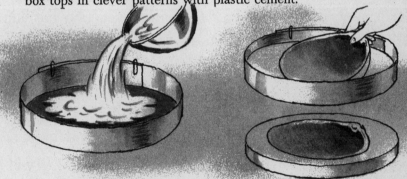

You can make an ash tray by pouring cement into a circular cardboard form (like the one used for casting animal tracks), and setting a clam shell into the wet mix. Let the cement dry, remove the form and then paint the cement any color you desire.

Things To Do With Driftwood: Sun-silvered gnarled branches washed up on beaches from far-away romantic shores can be used for decorative objects in any home. Pick your pieces carefully. For instance, find one which, when you flatten the bottom a little, might make an interesting central figure around which you can arrange flowers for a table centerpiece, or put in a planting box. Some lend themselves to lamp-making.

Make A Salt Water Aquarium: Nearly everyone has kept tropical fish or goldfish at one time or another. But not many people have thought about making a salt water aquarium. You need the same kind of equipment that is used for a fresh-water aquarium—tank, aerator, and dip net. But ocean water must be used—not just salted fresh water. Instead of green plants, you can have odd sea vegetation, dead coral and strange ocean bottom creatures to decorate the tank—things like starfish, small snails, and anemones (uh-*nem*-uh-nees) that sit on the bottom and wave their tentacles.

More curious than the decorations are the small sea *fish* that go into the tank. There's the lumpy little filefish with fluorescent green eyes; and an odd, squarish fellow called the "four-eyed-butterfly fish," named for the black spots on his back that look more like eyes than his real ones. You'll want a tiny one-inch, boxlike creature called a "cowfish," with a head just like a cow's—horns and all—and ballast tanks that enable him to go up and down in the water like a submarine. Seahorses are real curiosities for any salt water aquarium. After a female seahorse lays eggs, she gives them to the male seahorse who puts them in a pouch on his vest and hatches them out.

Almost any small sea creature from the nearest beach is a candidate for a salt water aquarium—little hermit crabs, jellyfish, mussels and baby horseshoe crabs. Dozens of fellows easily scooped from the tidal water along the sandy coves will do.

There's one thing to remember about a salt water aquarium: Once you have a bowl of real ocean water, it must *not* be freshened with new ocean water. You freshen it with *fresh* water as the ocean water evaporates. Why? Because the minerals in the sea water don't evaporate. If you added ocean water, you'd soon have so much salt in the tank that the creatures would die. About once every three months or so, however, it's a good idea to throw out the entire tankful and start over with a fresh load of clean ocean water.

The seas are especially exciting to scientists because they still hold many undiscovered secrets. Only recently have men been able to explore the ocean's deepest trenches in strange craft like the Bathyscaphe (bath-iss-*kaff*), and to flash bright lights through the stygian darkness more than five miles deep to gaze at scenes no human eye has ever seen. Deep sea nets of oceanographers, as sea scientists are called, are bringing up new, unknown creatures all the time. New instruments are detecting great rivers deep in the ocean that may have a great deal to do with the world's weather. And pretty soon, a group of American scientists are going to drill a hole deep into the floor of the sea, in order to bring up samples of the rock that makes up the earth's basement.

With all that we think we know about this old globe on which we live, people with enough curiosity to keep poking around are forever discovering new things that were never suspected before. So little is known about the ocean that even you and I collecting shells, and catching fish, may turn up something new and exciting if we are smart enough to recognize it. That's why it is important to study the specimens we collect and read up on them. It was a sharp-eyed amateur who spotted an odd fish in a fisherman's catch a few years ago. He investigated it with the help of authorities, and discovered that it was a prehistoric fish called Ceolocanth (*seal*-oh-kanth), which scientists had thought to be long extinct. Since then, many other specimens of this "living fossil" have been hauled up off the coasts of Africa—still primitive, but very much alive.

Although the unexplored seas offer a tremendous challenge, there's still plenty of room for fresh discovery all around us. It wasn't so long ago that a young hiker in Vermont stumbled across a spectacular collection of fossil dinosaur tracks near Lake Champlain. While you may not be fortunate enough to turn up anything as glamorous as that on your hikes, you'll be surprised at the real excitement that can come from the discovery of the first deer or raccoon tracks that you find and are able to identify. Parting a bush to see an oriole's nest dangling above you, spying an unusual moth or butterfly, finding a cluster of owl pellets beneath an old tree, turning up an old Indian arrowhead in a ploughed field—all of these things will provide a genuine thrill once you know what you are looking for and what you have found.

And if this book has helped in the smallest way to give you some of the flavor or fun and adventure that is to be found in nature study, then it will have served its purpose. Good luck, and happy hunting.

BOOKS TO READ

Animals

Audubon's Animals, edited by Alice Ford, published by Thomas Y. Crowell Co.

Parade of the Animals, by Robert Hegner, published by Macmillan Company

Trees and Leaves

Forest Wonders, by Eva Knox Evans, published by Capitol Publishing Co.

Trees and Trails, by Clarence Hylander, published by Macmillan Company

What Tree is That?, by J. E. Potzger, published by Kenworthy Educational Service, Inc.

The American Book of the Woods, by David S. Marx, published by the Botanic Publishing Co.

Birds, Nests and Feathers

Adventure Book of Birds, by William Jerr, Capitol Publishing Co.

Field Guide to the Birds (Eastern or Western), by Roger Tory Peterson, published by Houghton, Mifflin Co.

Audubon Bird Guide (Eastern or Western), by Richard Pough, published by Doubleday & Co.

Bird Nests, by Richard Headstrom, published by Ives, Washburn Inc.

Ponds and Streams

The Adventure Book of Underwater Life, by Dr. Carlton Ray, Capitol Publishing Co.

The Underwater Zoo, by Theodore McClintock, published by Vanguard Press, Inc.

The Pond World, by C. H. Lawrence and Esther Bjoland, Garden City Publishing Co.

Insects and Butterflies

The Adventure Book of Insects, by Alice Gray, Capitol Publishing Co.

Field Guide to Butterflies of North America, by Alexander Klots, published by Houghton, Mifflin Co.

The Butterfly Book, by William J. Holland, Doubleday & Co.

How to Know the Insects, by H. E. Jaques, W. C. Brown Co.

The Insect Guide, by R. B. Swain, published by Doubleday & Co.

Field Book of Insects, by F. E. Lutz, published by G. P. Putnam's Sons

INDEX

Answers to questions on page 1

Chapter 1
1. plaster cast
2. cloven
3. danger signal
4. night
5. pads
6. hearing; 40
7. gray fox
8. weasel
9. 15
10. good
11. tomato juice
12. otter
13. muskrat
14. Opossum
15. don't; do
16. long; short

Chapter 2
1. hollow; bones
2. winter
3. summer
4. refracted

Chapter 3
1. amphibans; shallow

2. salamander
3. amphibians
4. newt
5. not
6. nest
7. impression, print

Chapter 4
1. outside; three; six
2. compound
3. walking stick
4. a quarter of a mile
5. praying mantis
6. the wind
7. animals

Chapter 5
1. sedimentary, igneous, metamorphic
2. crystals
3. fossils
4. fluorescent

Chapter 6
1. Buoyancy
2. salt, fresh
3. surface tension
4. mollusks
5. a storm